DWIGHT D.

EISENHOWER

DWIGHT D. EISENHOWER

DWIGHT D. EISENHOWER

SAMUEL BRENNER, *Book Editor*

DANIEL LEONE, *President*
BONNIE SZUMSKI, *Publisher*
SCOTT BARBOUR, *Managing Editor*
JAMES D. TORR, *Series Editor*

GREENHAVEN PRESS
SAN DIEGO, CALIFORNIA

THOMSON
─────★─────
™
GALE

Detroit • New York • San Diego • San Francisco
Boston • New Haven, Conn. • Waterville, Maine
London • Munich

Every effort has been made to trace the owners of copyrighted material. The articles in this volume may have been edited for content, length, and/or reading level. The titles have been changed to enhance the editorial purpose.

No part of this book may be reproduced or used in any form or by any means, electrical, mechanical, or otherwise, including, but not limited to, photocopy, recording, or any information storage and retrieval system without prior written permission from the publisher.

Library of Congress Cataloging-in-Publication Data

Dwight D. Eisenhower / by Samuel Brenner, book editor.
    p. cm. — (Presidents and their decisions)
    ISBN 0-7377-1110-8 (hardback : alk. paper) — ISBN 0-7377-1109-4 (pbk. : alk. paper)
    1. Eisenhower, Dwight D. (Dwight David), 1890–1969—Juvenile literature. 2. Presidents—United States—Biography—Juvenile literature. 3. United States—Politics and government—1953–1961—Juvenile literature. [1. Eisenhower, Dwight D. (Dwight David), 1890–1969. 2. Presidents. 3. United States—Politics and government—1953–1961.] I. Title. II. Series.

E836 .B745 2002
973.921'092—dc21   2001008361

Cover photo: © Bettmann/CORBIS
Library of Congress, 21, 31, 33

CONTENTS

CHAPTER 1: CONTAINING COMMUNISM

Chapter 2: Avoiding War in Vietnam

Chapter 3: McCarthyism and Presidential Silence

decision in *Brown v. Board,* but ultimately resolved to obey the Court's ruling.

FOREWORD

"**T**HE PRESIDENCY OF THE UNITED STATES IS OFTEN DE-scribed as the most powerful office in the world," writes Forrest McDonald in *The American Presidency: An Intellectual History.* "In one sense this description is accurate," he says, "for even casual decisions made in the White House can affect the lives of millions of people." But McDonald also notes that presidential power "is restrained by the countervailing power of Congress, the courts, the bureaucracy, popular opinion, the news media, and state and local governments. What presidents do have is awesome responsibilities combined with unique opportunities to persuade others to do their bidding—opportunities enhanced by the possibility of dispensing favors, by the mystique of presidential power, and by the aura of monarchy that surrounds the president."

The way various presidents have used the complex power of their office is the subject of Greenhaven Press's Presidents and Their Decisions series. Each volume in the series examines one particular president and the key decisions he made while in office.

Some presidential decisions have been made in a relatively brief period of time, as with Abraham Lincoln's suspension of the writ of habeus corpus at the start of the Civil War. Others were refined as they were implemented over a period of years, as was the case with Franklin Delano Roosevelt's struggle to lead the country out of the Great Depression. Some presidential actions are generally lauded by historians—for example, Lyndon Johnson's support of the civil rights movement in the 1960s—while others have been condemned—such as Richard Nixon's efforts, from 1972 to 1974, to cover up the involvement of his aides in the Watergate scandal.

Most of the truly history-making presidential decisions, though, remain the subject of intense scrutiny and historical debate. Many of these were made during a time of war or other crisis, in which a president was forced to risk either spectacular success or devastating failure. Examples include Lincoln's much-scrutinized handling of the crisis at Fort Sumter, the first conflict of the Civil War; FDR's efforts to aid the European Allies at the beginning of World War II; Harry Truman's controversial decision to use the atomic bomb in order to end that conflict; and Lyndon Johnson's fateful decision to escalate the war in Vietnam.

Each volume in the Presidents and Their Decisions series devotes a full chapter to each of the president's key decisions. The essays in each chapter, most written by presidential historians and biographers, offer a range of perspectives on the president and his actions. Some provide background on the political, social, and economic factors behind a particular decision. Others critique the president's performance, offering a negative or positive appraisal. Essays have been chosen for their concise and engaging presentation of the facts, and each is preceded by a straightforward summary of the article's content.

In addition to the articles, these books include extensive material to help the student researcher. An opening essay provides both a brief biography of the president and an overview of the events that occurred during his time in office. A chronology also helps readers keep track of the dates of specific events. A comprehensive index and an annotated table of contents aid readers in quickly locating material of interest, and an extensive bibliography serves as a launching point for further research. Finally, an appendix of primary historical documents provides a sampling of the president's most important speeches, as well as some of his contemporaries' criticisms.

Greenhaven Press's Presidents and Their Decisions series will help students gain a deeper understanding of the decisions made by some of the most influential leaders in American history.

Dwight D. Eisenhower:
A Biography

"I HATE WAR," DECLARED DWIGHT DAVID EISENHOWER in 1946, "as only a soldier who has lived it can, only as one who has seen its brutality, its stupidity."[1] This sentiment might seem unusual coming from the man who had commanded the most powerful military alliance in history during the greatest and most destructive war the world has yet seen. In fact, however, this comment demonstrates a key characteristic of a man who would go on to serve as president of the United States of America: a refusal to adopt a position or an ideology simply because it was expected of him. Speaking in 1956, the president explained "I have one yardstick by which I test every major problem—and that yardstick is: Is it good for America?"[2] While this patriotic boast was clearly intended to strengthen Eisenhower's popularity (it was, after all, made as part of a political speech), Eisenhower's record as president demonstrates that he routinely acted in ways that ran against the desires of the Republican Party and of his closest supporters. Some of his actions, such as his decision to send federal troops into Little Rock, Arkansas, in 1954, were ultimately justified, while others, such as his decision not to speak out against the excesses of McCarthyism, have been called into question or else condemned by history. Very few, however, would claim that Eisenhower acted rashly, or that he was indecisive on important questions. When he acted, he moved with speed and authority—and when he chose not to act, he did so knowing that his decisions would have serious consequences.

From its inception as a nation, the United States has had a tradition of generals serving as presidents. George Washington, Andrew Jackson, William Henry Harrison,

Zachary Taylor, Ulysses S. Grant—all had commanded American troops in battle and gone on to win election to the highest office in the land. As presidents, these men acted as they had been trained in the military, and their decisions very often reflected the military's mindset and traditions. Eisenhower was no exception: His military training and background left an indelible mark on his character. As an officer, Eisenhower learned to make decisions quickly and to stand by those decisions. When he single-handedly made the decision to proceed with the D day invasion of Normandy during the Second World War in the face of dangerously poor weather conditions, he first listened to competing arguments and then simply declared, "Okay, we'll go."[3] Perhaps more importantly, Eisenhower was willing to stand behind the decisions that he made so adroitly. Even as Allied troops were preparing to hit the beaches on the day of the invasion, Eisenhower was carrying in his pocket a crumpled piece of paper on which he had written a message that he had prepared in case the invasion proved to be a failure. "Our landings in the Cherbourg-Havre area have failed to gain a satisfactory foothold," read the short note, "and I have withdrawn the troops. My decision to attack at this time and place was based upon the best information available. The troops, the air and the navy did all that bravery and devotion to duty could do. If any blame or fault attaches to the attempt, it is mine."[4] Eisenhower brought his ability to make and support military decisions to the presidency, and so he was unflinchingly able to send troops to keep order in Little Rock and to withhold critical U.S. military support from French forces fighting at Dien Bien Phu.

Eisenhower was a man of contrasts. He was a general who hated war, an elected official who disdained politics, a southern gentleman who enforced school desegregation, a states' rights advocate who dispatched federal troops to the capital of Arkansas, a former commander of the U.S. armed forces who warned the nation about the evils of spending money on military equipment—as both a man and as a president, Eisenhower defies easy characterization. Several points, however, do stand out. In addition to his desire to do what was best for America, Eisenhower felt strongly that it was the responsibility of the president to guide the nation and to stay "above the fray" of partisan politics. He also believed that in order to be successful the nation would need to avoid the path of extremism. "The middle of the road is all of the usable surface," he declared. "The extremes, right and left, are in the gutters."[5] Finally, Eisenhower firmly believed that it was necessary to face and defeat world communism, and that the way to defeat communism was to encourage the spread of American democracy and economic power throughout the world. "Unless we can put things in the hands of people who are starving to death," he explained, "we can never lick communism."[6]

In studying famous leaders, historians cannot afford to ignore the mistakes that those leaders made, the misjudgments of which they are guilty, and the morally ambiguous or indeed morally wrong positions that they supported. Again, Eisenhower is no exception; as both a man and as a political leader, he made some poor choices. It appears, for instance, that during the war he carried on a lengthy extramarital affair with his Australian driver and secretary, Kay Summersby. Less personally, the president was critical of desegregation and possessed a mixed record on civil rights issues. In studying Eisenhower, therefore, it is important to be aware of and to understand all of the facets of his personality, both positive and negative. But whatever his mistakes, Eisenhower is a vitally important figure in the history of the United States.

The Young Eisenhower

Dwight Eisenhower was born to David Jacob and Ida Elizabeth Stover Eisenhower in Denison, Texas, on October 14,

1890. The third of seven sons, Eisenhower was not considered especially intelligent or driven to succeed. He was a dutiful son and a hard worker, and though he was somewhat gifted in sports, by all accounts he had a very normal childhood. The Eisenhower family was originally from Kansas, but Dwight's father had moved the family to Texas following the failure and bankruptcy of the general store he had owned and managed for three years. Two years after Dwight was born, David Eisenhower found steady work at the Belle Springs Creamery in Abilene, and so the entire family moved back to Kansas. Eisenhower's unpretentious origins continued to affect him throughout his time in the U.S. military and in the White House. Even when he rose to the office of president, at some level he remained an ordinary man from Kansas.

Eisenhower graduated from Abilene's high school in 1910, having concentrated on sports, with little idea of what he wanted to do. He and one of his brothers arranged to each spend one year working in order to pay for the other to go to college, and so Eisenhower found a job at the Belle Springs Creamery while his brother went off to school. Soon, however, Eisenhower was convinced by a friend to apply to the military service academies, where the tuition was covered by the government. In July 1911 Eisenhower took the entrance exams for both Annapolis and the Military Academy at West Point. The future president received high marks on both exams, and intended to attend the Naval Academy until he found out that at twenty years of age he was too old to enter. Eisenhower was not discouraged, and instead sought and received an appointment to West Point from Kansas senator Joseph Bristow.

Life in the Military

When Eisenhower entered West Point in 1911, he found himself in a very different environment than the one he was used to. Surrounded by articulate and accomplished peers, Eisenhower again chose to focus on sports. He was not unintelligent, but he preferred activity to reading, and found studying academic subjects thoroughly boring. Even as president, Eisenhower rarely read anything other than military history and westerns, which he devoured voraciously. In his junior year Eisenhower's prowess as a football player began to receive national attention, but then he suffered serious damage to his knee after a riding instructor forced the cadet to mount and dismount his horse hundreds of times in a single afternoon as a training exercise. In his senior year the future president was relegated to coaching junior level teams instead of playing on the varsity squad. His physical aspirations challenged, Eisenhower rededicated himself to his course of study, and ultimately finished in the top third of his graduating class.

Eisenhower graduated from West Point in 1915, was immediately commissioned as a second lieutenant, and in September was sent to join the 19th Infantry at Fort Sam Houston in Texas. At Fort Houston, Eisenhower fell in love with Mamie Geneva Doud, the daughter of a well-off businessman. Within months the couple was engaged, despite Mamie's own concerns about marrying a career army officer. Eisenhower and Mamie Doud were married on July 1, 1916, the same day Eisenhower received a promotion to first lieutenant. The newly married couple settled into life at Fort Houston, and after a year Mamie gave birth to a boy, Doud Dwight Eisenhower.

While the couple was still settling into married life, Eisenhower and his fellow officers began to focus their attention on the development of the First World War in Europe. It was a very interesting time for the United States: President Wilson had just been reelected by promising that the United States would not become involved in the conflict. "We must," the president explained, "be neutral in thought and deed."[7] Still, as the Germans intensified their efforts to destroy British shipping with torpedoes launched from submarines, the United States became entangled in the controversy. In April 1915 German U-boats had sunk the RMS *Lusitania* and killed thousands of civilians—including hundreds of Americans. Although the Germans agreed to rein in their submarine forces following the *Lusitania* incident, by the beginning of 1917 the German high command decided that in order to win the war it would need to wage unrestricted submarine warfare. President Wilson announced that the United States could not abide Germany's use of submarine warfare, and so in April 1917 the United States declared war upon Germany.

Obviously the declaration of war had a serious impact upon American military officers. As the government struggled to recruit and train the millions of men necessary to support American involvement in the war, Eisenhower's fellow officers found themselves in command of powerful new formations with orders to proceed to Europe. However, despite repeated requests, Eisenhower was not assigned to lead troops overseas, but instead suffered through a series of critical yet boring training assignments in the United States. After serving with the 57th Infantry in Texas, Eisenhower reported for duty as an instructor at the Officers' Training Camp at Fort Oglethorpe, Georgia, and then as an instructor at the Army Service Schools at Fort Leavenworth, Kansas. Eisenhower then organized a battalion of engineers in Maryland, after which he assumed command of Camp Colt, Pennsylvania, a tank training center, and finally commanded Tank Corps troops at Camp Dix, New Jersey, and Fort Benning, Georgia.

For his work at Camp Colt, Eisenhower received the Distinguished Service Medal and served with the temporary rank of lieutenant colonel (he reverted to the rank of captain after the end of the war), but he nevertheless felt as though he had missed the war. For a professional soldier such as Eisenhower, failure to serve in combat or to command combat troops was a serious blow. He and Mamie

Doud were dealt another blow when, immediately following the cessation of hostilities, the young Doud Dwight Eisenhower died after contracting a fever. Although a second son, John Sheldon Doud, was born to the Eisenhowers in August 1922, Eisenhower's spirits were clearly at a low ebb. He remained in the military, but as he later admitted, he had lost his sense of mission and any desire to do more than earn a steady living.

In the middle of 1922, Eisenhower was ordered to report to the Panama Canal Zone, where he served as the executive officer of Camp Gaillard. It was in Panama, as Eisenhower himself later recounted, that the future president finally began to apply himself to the serious study of international affairs, military history, and strategy. Eisenhower's commanding officer treated the still-young Kansan as a student as well as an officer, and required Eisenhower to read and report on books and strategic analyses of historical campaigns. Gradually Eisenhower's interest was piqued, and by the time Eisenhower left the Panama Canal Zone in 1924 his superior could recommend him wholeheartedly for admission to the army's Command and General Staff School, the institution in which all of the U.S. Army's future high-ranking officers were trained. Eisenhower had finally found his calling: The normally indifferent student graduated in June 1926 with honors, the first in academic standing in a class of 245. From that moment on, Eisenhower's future as one of the leaders of the U.S. military was virtually assured.

World War II

The 1920s and 1930s were years of growing political extremism in and increasing international tension among the largest and most powerful nations in the world. The period ultimately culminated in the Second World War. War had seemed imminent to some observers since the end of the First World War. At the Versailles conference of

1919, the victors of World War I had forced Germany to pay war reparations and decided who would remain in control of colonial territories formerly ruled by Germany and her allies. France and Britain, for example, used the conference to strengthen their own positions in Indochina and India, respectively. Far from solving the many problems of the First World War, the Versailles conference simply exacerbated the disagreements and nationalist urges that had contributed to the initial conflict.

In many ways the Second World War flowed as a direct result from the Treaty of Versailles: The reparations that Britain and France forced Germany to pay, for instance, bankrupted and embittered the German people, contributed to the worldwide economic depression that ultimately struck the United States at the end of the 1920s and helped the Austrian-born Fascist dictator Adolf Hitler to assume power in Germany. Hitler, the leader of the National Socialists ("Nazis"), was a brilliant political manipulator and enormously charismatic speaker who brutally presided over Germany's rebirth as an industrial and military power during the period. He also perpetrated some of

Dwight D. Eisenhower

the worst war crimes in history. By the late 1930s Hitler had assumed dictatorial powers in Germany and had set in motion his horrific plans to eliminate through genocide the millions of Jews (and also Gypsies and Socialists) living in Europe while waging aggressive warfare in order to subjugate the peoples of the world under the "Third Reich" of German power. By the time Germany moved against Czechoslovakia in 1938, many leaders in the American military felt that the United States was destined to become involved in a worldwide conflict.

Although the U.S. military leadership was deeply concerned by the development of fascism in Germany, Italy, and Japan during this period, much of the American population was still determined to avoid becoming entangled in the seemingly never-ending problems of Europe. American officers thus spent the 1920s and 1930s in a shrunken, ill-funded military that had no clear international mission. In response to the declining reputation of the services, many professional officers left the military while others tended to focus inwardly on their own professional development and on the expansion of American hegemony overseas in Hawaii, China, and the Philippines. Eisenhower was no exception: After his outstanding performance at the Command and General Staff School, the future president found that he was being considered for promotion by his military superiors. During the next two years, he served with the 24th Infantry and as a staff officer with the American Battle Monuments Commission before reporting to the Army War College. Eisenhower returned to the commission after graduation from the college, but then reported for duty as assistant executive in the office of the assistant secretary of war. By the mid-1930s, Eisenhower was serving in the office of General Marshall, the chief of staff of the army, and in September 1935 he was ordered to report to General Douglas MacArthur to serve as the assistant to the military adviser of the Commonwealth of the Philippine Islands. While Eisenhower disliked duty in the Philippines, his service there again brought him to Marshall's attention. When Marshall began looking for young officers to help bring the U.S. Army to the level it would need to be at in order to protect American interests against the Axis Powers (Germany, Italy, and Japan), he immediately settled upon Eisenhower.

During the Second World War, Eisenhower was promoted over seven times in four years. At the time of the Japanese attack on Pearl Harbor in 1941, Eisenhower was serving as the chief of staff of the Third Army Division. Within a week, he was appointed deputy chief of the division, and within two months he was brought to Washington to serve as the chief of the War Plans Division of the War Department General Staff. By June 1942, Eisenhower was serving as commanding general of the European Theater. Five months later he commanded the successful American forces landing in North Africa. Within two years, he was commanding the Allied troops landing in Normandy, and within three years he was accepting the surrender of the German government. Eisenhower's leadership during the war was nothing short of incredible, and he became a personal hero to millions of American soldiers and their families. These ties would assist him several years later in his run for the presidency.

Running for President

After the war Eisenhower found himself a folk hero in the United States. Wherever he went he was greeted with parades and speeches, and both political parties scrambled to enlist him as a candidate for the 1948 presidential campaign. Eisenhower, however, was not interested in becoming a politician. Instead, he first served as the Allied commander in occupied Germany, and then accepted the position of U.S. Army chief of staff (the highest-ranking position in the U.S. Army). In 1948, he became the president of Columbia University in New York. Although the general was still no academic, he felt that the presidency of a major university would give him a pulpit from which to discuss domestic and foreign policy. Eisenhower soon found out that he was unsuited for the academic life. He was simply not qualified to lead a major university and found himself constantly at odds with the faculty.

Eisenhower was rescued from this situation when President Harry Truman asked him in 1950 to assume command of NATO forces in Europe. (NATO is the North Atlantic Treaty Organization, the organization set up to oppose the spread of the Soviet Union after the Second World War.) The general once gain assumed a critical role on the world stage. Still, however, Eisenhower refused to commit either to a political party or to a presidential run. He might, he explained to the anxious politicians who came to visit him, accept a draft by a convention, but he would not ask to be relieved of his position in order to campaign. As the 1952 election drew closer, however, it became apparent that in order to win a nomination Eisenhower would have to go back on his words. That year Eisenhower asked President Truman to relieve him of his duties, and the former general immediately began to campaign for the Republican nomination.

In both of the campaigns Eisenhower ran as a presidential candidate, he emerged quickly as the most popular candidate. His simple and direct campaign slogan—"I Like Ike"—suited him. (For the second campaign, Eisenhower staffers printed up millions of "I Still Like Ike" buttons instead.) Throughout his campaign, Eisenhower emphasized issues such as the spread of the Soviet Union, the importance of developing nuclear weapons as a deterrent, and the necessity of ending the war in Korea. The American public remembered him as the man who had won the war in Europe, and in both 1952 and 1956 Eisenhower handily defeated Adlai Stevenson, the Democratic nominee.

Upon taking office in 1953, Eisenhower found himself faced with several pressing domestic concerns. Eisenhower's forte was clearly foreign policy, but as president, before he could turn his attention to the development of world communism, he needed to address serious questions concerning civil rights and desegregation, to appoint a new chief justice of the Supreme Court, to guide the American educational system through a period of explosive growth and development, and even to weigh in on the question of whether Hawaii and Alaska should be admitted to the Union as states. The most pressing problem facing the new president upon taking office, however, was how to deal with an abrasive demagogic junior senator from Wisconsin.

Dealing with McCarthy

"Today we are engaged in a final, all-out battle between communistic atheism and Christianity," declared Senator Joseph McCarthy on February 9, 1950. "The modern champions of communism have selected this as the time. And, ladies and gentlemen, the chips are down—they are truly down."[8] With these words, McCarthy—who had until then been an unimportant and even shady character in Washington—stepped out of the shadows and into the limelight of American national politics. Within two years he was one of the most powerful men in the country. During the years he was active on the national scene, he changed the way Americans viewed individuals in government service and forced Eisenhower to take a stand on the question of executive privilege (a special right of the president). The way Eisenhower dealt with McCarthy demonstrates clearly how Eisenhower conceived of his role as president.

Joseph McCarthy was an unsuccessful lawyer from Wisconsin who managed to win election as a circuit court judge in 1940. He resigned his office and joined the marines after the attack on Pearl Harbor in 1941, and for the remainder of the war held a desk job and several times flew in training flights. He was never in combat, and was never wounded. In 1946, however, when he returned from the war to run for the U.S. Senate seat from Wisconsin, he portrayed himself as a war hero—his posters depicted him in full flight uniform toting machine-gun ammunition. Within a few years, McCarthy found himself in serious trouble, under investigation for taking bribes and for falsifying his war record.

It was when sitting with his staff in 1950, trying to devise some way to stave off the investigators, that McCarthy seized upon the idea of attacking communists within the U.S. government. He had not been a particularly staunch anticommunist before 1950, but beginning with his speech to the Women's Republican Club in Wheeling, West Virginia, in February, McCarthy became the single most important voice for anticommunists in the United States. "While I cannot take the time to name all the men in the State Department who have been named as members of the Communist Party and members of a spy ring," he explained to his audience, "I have here in my hand a list of 205."[9] Although the list of 205 quickly shrank to 81—McCarthy never showed it to anyone—the senator's comments become more strident and more insistent. After the Republicans won control of the Senate in 1953, McCarthy became the chairman of the Senate Permanent Subcommittee on Investigations, and was chiefly responsible for launching the "Red Scare" of the 1950s.

"Are you now, or have you ever been, a member of the Communist Party?" The question was made famous by McCarthy's House Committee on Un-American Activities. Witnesses who refused to answer were censured, while those who chose to respond were asked to name any others they knew who might be involved in the Communist Party. Those named were often fired from their jobs, asked to leave schools, and evicted from their apartments. Hollywood was hit particularly hard, as many actors, screenwriters, and directors were accused and subsequently "blacklisted," or prevented from working. Despite having almost no evidence that any communist conspiracy was present in the United States, McCarthy continued to expand the hearings, disrupting numerous lives and shocking millions of Americans. While some Americans, disgusted with the silence in Washington concerning McCarthy's methods, chose to leave the country, others instead began to fight back by asking their elected representatives to rein in the marauding Wisconsin senator. Many turned to Eisenhower and asked him to take a public stand against McCarthy's actions, rhetoric, and demagoguery.

Eisenhower was not one of McCarthy's admirers, and indeed regarded him with distaste. As McCarthy's actions and accusations became more strident and dangerous, Eisenhower was faced with the question of whether he should make some public statement. Eisenhower chose not to condemn the senator publicly. Despite his personal feelings about McCarthy, Eisenhower firmly believed that it was his responsibility as president to stay above the fray of partisan politics. The president, he explained, had no business making any comments about the senators and representatives chosen by the people of a particular state; it was simply not his place. Eisenhower held to this belief even as McCarthy's attacks became more and more absurd. Ultimately, Eisenhower only publicly challenged McCarthy on one issue. When the senator sought to question the presidential staff, Eisenhower exploded, declaring that any staffer who agreed to testify would be fired instantly. With this declaration that the president's staff and actions were above questioning, Eisenhower laid the foundation for presidential claims of "executive privilege," a legal doctrine that protects the confidentiality of the president's conversations with advisers. (This doctrine later became pivotal during the administrations of Richard Nixon and Bill Clinton, as those presidents attempted to hide serious indiscretions from public scrutiny.)

McCarthy's downfall proved to be as incredible as his rise to power had been a few years earlier. In April 1954 McCarthy focused his attacks on Secretary of the Army Robert T. Stevens, whom he accused of concealing evidence of espionage activities at Fort Monmouth, New Jersey. In response, the army accused McCarthy of attempting to obtain preferential treatment for one of his aides, who was then serving in the military. McCarthy's committee convened hearings, and ABC chose to broadcast live, gavel-to-gavel coverage to the nation. For six weeks, the American public watched McCarthy face off against Joseph N. Welch, a refined Boston lawyer who was serving as the army's special counsel. The climax of the hearings came on June 9, when McCarthy verbally attacked another Boston lawyer, a young colleague of Welch's. "Have you no sense of decency, sir, at long last? Have you left no sense of decency?"[10] shot back a furious Welch. As the gallery erupted in applause, McCarthy turned to an aide with an expression of bewilderment and wondered what had happened. Within months the U.S. Senate voted to condemn McCarthy, and the reign of McCarthyism came to an end.

Desegregation and Civil Rights

Even as controversy swirled around the Army-McCarthy hearings, Eisenhower was focusing much of his attention on another critical national issue: desegregation. The question was whether the federal government could or should require that black children be permitted to attend what had previously been all-white schools, all of which were located in southern states. The debate was not new to Eisenhower's presidency: It had been a divisive issue in American society for decades, and it was clear that it would need to be resolved eventually. The controversy was inflamed in 1954, however, by the Supreme Court's decision in *Brown v. Board of Education of Topeka, Kansas*—a ruling that was largely the result of the work of Chief Justice Earl Warren.

Warren is considered one of the most important and influential chief justices ever to sit on the Supreme Court. He owed his appointment to Eisenhower, and so in a very real sense the changes that Warren wrought upon American society were the result of one of Eisenhower's decisions. Unlike many justices, Warren was a politician before his appointment to the Court. After serving as California's attorney general for several years, he was elected governor of California in 1942 after winning both the Republican and the Democratic primaries. Warren mounted a failed bid for the vice presidency in 1948, and was passed over by Eisenhower in favor of the more conservative Richard Nixon as a running mate in 1952. Eisenhower initially promised the Californian a cabinet position, but when Chief Justice Frederick Vinson died suddenly in 1953, Eisenhower decided to appoint Warren to the vacant position. Because the Senate was not in session at the time, Warren took up his duties immediately without waiting for confirmation hearings.

Eisenhower, the consummate moderate, considered carefully before appointing Warren to the bench. The one thing that the president did not want to do was to "rock the boat" by picking either an extreme liberal or a staunch conservative. The information the president had received on Warren seemed to indicate that the Californian fell somewhere in the middle. Eisenhower's older brother Edgar, a conservative lawyer, advised the president that Warren was a "leftist tool," while Eisenhower's younger brother Milton, then president of Pennsylvania State University, claimed that Warren was the spokesman for extreme right-wing conservatives. Eisenhower essentially decided to split the difference, and appointed Warren after concluding that any candidate feared by both the left and the right would surely be a safe, stable justice. Within months, a horrified Eisenhower realized that he had appointed an activist to the bench. Appointing Warren, Eisenhower would later declare, "was the biggest damn-fool mistake I ever made."[11]

Perhaps Warren's most important moment came with the 1954 *Brown* decision. The question of desegregation dated back to the years immediately following the Civil War. After Reconstruction (the rebuilding of the war-torn South), many of the southern states instituted laws prohibiting African Americans from using the same facilities as

Caucasians. Nonwhites were forced to ride in separate railroad cars, to use separate bathrooms, and to attend separate schools. The Supreme Court had officially condoned such laws in 1896 in the case of *Plessy v. Ferguson*, in which eight of the justices ruled that segregation laws were constitutional, as long as both whites and nonwhites had access to "separate but equal" facilities. In the *Brown* ruling, however, the Court reversed itself and ruled unanimously that "separate educational facilities are inherently unequal." The justices ordered that states with segregation rules take immediate steps to consolidate the segregated schools in their districts. The federal government, it was understood, would be responsible for enforcing the Court's decision.

Like much of history, the debate over desegregation and over the *Brown* ruling was not as simple and one-sided as it first appears. Contrary to popular belief, not all of those who opposed desegregation were first and foremost racists. Indeed, even some African American leaders, anxious to preserve all-black schools which were a major source of pride for local communities, objected to the forced desegregation. Other opponents of desegregation were more concerned with the constitutional implications of the Supreme Court ruling and of Eisenhower's involvement. These critics argued that no matter the justification, the Supreme Court could not and should not rule on matters internal to the states. The proper jurisdiction of the federal government, they argued, is strictly limited to those powers enumerated in the Constitution—to "provide for the common defense, promote the general welfare, and secure the blessings of liberty to ourselves and our posterity." Still, it is clear that most of the opponents of desegregation were motivated by racial arguments, and that the Court's decision was the first step in fixing a system that grossly discriminated against African Americans.

The *Brown* decision left Eisenhower in a serious quandary. A southerner by birth, the president was uncomfortable with civil rights questions. While there is no evidence to suggest that Eisenhower discriminated against individuals because of their race, it is clear that as president he ignored several opportunities to address the systematic discrimination against African Americans in the South. Eisenhower personally disagreed with the *Brown* decision; he felt that the question of desegregation should be left up to the states.

In 1957, however, the president was forced to take action to support a Supreme Court decision with which he disagreed. The segregationist governor of Arkansas, Orval Faubus, was wavering on his announced intention to support integration, and his public comments were stirring up emotions in Little Rock. When Faubus declared his intention to prevent the desegregation of Little Rock's schools, the town broke into violence. Vacationing in Rhode Island, Eisenhower learned of the situation and ordered federal

Escorted by federal troops, a group of African American students leaves Central High School in Little Rock, Arkansas.

troops into Little Rock to restore order. The president then rushed back to the White House in order to address the nation. Many Americans were shocked that Eisenhower, a known supporter of states' rights, would send federal troops into a state capital. Eisenhower, however, quickly dismissed any suggestion that his actions as president would be affected by his own personal political beliefs. "Our personal opinions about the decision have no bearing on the matter of enforcement," the president explained. "Mob rule cannot be allowed to override the decisions of our courts."[12] With this announcement, Eisenhower made it clear that his primary responsibility as president was to enforce the laws of the country. To Eisenhower the office of the president was far more important than the beliefs of the individual who temporarily occupied the office.

Foreign Policy

Although Eisenhower was forced to deal with many domestic issues while in office, the ex-general's forte was clearly foreign policy. He had recently finished serving as the highest-ranking officer in NATO, he was used to meeting with world leaders, and he was well aware of the growing rift between the United States and the Soviet Union. Rarely has an American president been so well qualified to deal with foreign affairs and to guide the United States through the often treacherous waters of international relations.

Eisenhower's overriding concern as president was the growing power of world communism. Communism had been expanding throughout Europe since before World War II—indeed much of the wartime conflict between Germany and the Soviet Union was due to the ideological conflict between fascism and communism. Like most Americans, Eisenhower believed strongly that communism was essentially evil. The primary responsibility of the United States on the world stage, he thought, must be to stop the spread of communism. To assist him in managing

Secretary of State John Foster Dulles and President Dwight Eisenhower discuss a plan to contain the spread of communism around the world.

affairs on the international stage, Eisenhower brought in John Foster Dulles as secretary of state. Together, Eisenhower and Dulles set about designing a national security apparatus that would be capable of countering communism around the world. The best way for the United States to fulfill its responsibility to the ideals of democracy, they maintained, was for American forces to prevent Soviet and communist forces from gaining any influence outside of the areas which they already controlled. This defensive strategy of "containment" was unusual in that it did not call for the U.S. military and Allied forces to attack the countries in which communism already held sway. Instead, both Eisenhower and Dulles sought to counter the spread of communism while avoiding becoming involved in serious military conflicts.

Even while he was focused on containing the spread of communism, however, Eisenhower was deeply concerned with what he saw as the increasing power of the "military-industrial complex" in the United States, the explosively rising costs of defense spending, and the decreasing efficiency and power of the U.S. military forces. Together, Eisenhower and Dulles instituted a defense policy known as the "New Look" to simultaneously decrease military costs while increasing U.S. reliance on weapons of mass destruction. The New Look can best be understood as a policy of "more bang for the buck." By decreasing U.S. conventional forces (ships, tanks, and troops), which cost huge sums of money to maintain, in favor of building more relatively inexpensive nuclear weapons, Eisenhower managed to reduce military spending while effectively increasing the power of U.S. forces.

The 1950s were years of enormous international tension and turmoil, and often required flexible and moderated responses in order to prevent events from spinning out of control. The hard-line stance of containment and the "all or nothing" nuclear threat of the New Look redefined America's military and strategic policies, but at the same time reduced the flexibility of the U.S. responses to international events and helped push all conflicts closer to threat of nuclear exchange. Eisenhower was certainly a foreign policy president, and as president he managed both to bring West Germany into the NATO alliance and to avoid any serious military conflict. But in the 1950s, as the United States and the Soviet Union were struggling to gain control of key strategic areas around the world, even Eisenhower's vaunted foreign policy skill simply was not sufficient all of the time.

Korea and Vietnam

While his tenure as president was marked by continuous strife and tension with the Soviet Union, Eisenhower was faced with four important specific foreign policy crises during his eight years in office. The first such crisis actually arose before the election, and before Eisenhower even decided to run for office. At the end of World War II the United States and its allies had taken up positions in South

Korea, where they provided military and political advice to the South Koreans, while the Soviets and their allies did the same in North Korea. In June 1950, however, North Korean forces stormed across the border between the two countries in an attempt to bring the South under the control of the North's Communist government. The South Koreans fought back with assistance from the United States and other allied countries (including Turkey and Australia), and by 1951 had succeeded in driving the North Koreans back past the 38th parallel. Once the South Korean and allied forces passed the parallel, however, Chinese forces entered the conflict and for the first time Chinese and American troops found themselves facing off on the battlefield. The war quickly degenerated into a series of bloody stalemates (over fifty thousand U.S. troops were killed in action in Korea), and by the time of the election the American public clearly wanted the conflict to be resolved. In response, Eisenhower made the Korean conflict a major campaign point: "If elected, I shall go to Korea,"[13] he declared in October. After the election, he fulfilled that promise, and while the final cease-fire was not signed for another six months, it seems clear that Eisenhower's enormous prestige with the American public, the military, and the international community helped smooth the way for the peace talks to proceed.

The second crisis came in 1954, and concerned the French colony of Indochina. Indochina (which would later become Vietnam) had been agitating for its independence from France for years before World War II. During the war, the French turned over control of the colony to Japan and many of the Vietnamese fighters who had been agitating for independence retreated to the forests and highlands, where they worked with U.S. operatives to destabilize the Japanese. Soon after the Japanese surrender, the Vietnamese, under their nationalist-Communist leader Ho Chi Minh, declared their independence by quoting the U.S.

Declaration of Independence. At the ceremony, U.S. operatives sat on the stage with Ho and U.S. aircraft flew in official formation overhead. Unfortunately, such cordial relations were not to continue, and for political and strategic reasons Presidents Truman and Eisenhower were forced to return control of Indochina to the French. Ho Chi Minh and his allies were deeply disappointed with this decision, and soon became engaged in a guerrilla war with the French expeditionary forces.

The French, who had been seriously embarrassed by their quick defeat at the beginning of World War II, by their subsequent collaboration with the Germans, and by the loss of their once-mighty empire, were determined to retain control of Indochina. Although they were being hurt by the guerrilla campaigns, they believed that there was no way for Ho and his fighters to win a significant victory—French forces were heavily armed, and routinely triumphed in set-piece battles. The French high command thus fixed upon the idea of instigating just such a traditional battle, presenting such a tempting target that the Vietminh (the name of Ho's forces) troops would be forced to attack en masse. The French built a large series of fortifications in the valley of Dien Bien Phu. They were certain that the Vietminh would never be able to attack in sufficient force to endanger the position, and that any such attack would simply result in hugely disproportionate losses for the Vietminh troops.

The French had not counted upon the dedication and perseverance of the Vietminh. Under the able command of General Vo Nguyen Giap, the Vietminh carried heavy artillery pieces through the hills to Dien Bien Phu. The French had not built their fortifications to withstand artillery bombardment, and soon found that their positions—and thousands of their elite troops—were in serious jeopardy. As the Vietminh closed in with wave assaults during a siege that lasted over fifty days, the French desperately turned to the United States for military assistance.

General Henri Navarre, the French commander, traveled to the United States and suggested that Eisenhower order a limited nuclear strike on the hills surrounding Dien Bien Phu. Other French officers suggested that the U.S. Air Force assist in driving the Vietminh off of the heights.

Eisenhower found himself in a serious quandary. On the one hand he needed French support in Europe to counter German reconstruction and Soviet pressure, and a French loss at Dien Bien Phu would have proved disastrous to such support. On the other hand he was personally sympathetic to the Vietnam cause and (after having been elected specifically to put an end to the Korean conflict) he was absolutely set on keeping U.S. troops out of land conflicts in Asia. In the end, Eisenhower decided not to allow the United States to become involved in the conflict. After a long siege, Dien Bien Phu fell, and France pulled out of Indochina, leaving the United States as the sole Western power to counter Communist influence in all of Southeast Asia. Nevertheless, with his decision not to become involved, Eisenhower kept the United States out of Vietnam. Later presidents would shoulder the blame for embroiling the United States in years of bloody conflict in Southeast Asia.

The Suez Canal Crisis and the U-2 Incident

The third major foreign policy crisis facing the Eisenhower administration involved the Suez Canal, one of the most important strategic and economic waterways in the world. Constructed during the middle of the nineteenth century, the canal provides the quickest access between the Mediterranean and the Indian Ocean. For much of the twentieth century, the canal was the preferred route for most oil-bearing ships heading to and from the Middle East. Since that time, the construction of supertankers that draw too much depth to utilize the canal has lessened its importance. During the 1950s, however, it was a vital lifeline for all of the nations of Europe.

In 1956, Israeli, French, and British forces conducted a raid designed to seize the Suez Canal from the Egyptians. The raid was planned in direct response to Egyptian efforts to restrict certain countries from using the canal and to the Egyptian decision to seize the canal from the French and British stockholders of the Suez Canal Company. The raid infuriated Eisenhower: He believed that Israel, France, and Great Britain had lied to him about their intentions and were exacerbating problems in the Middle East. Over a tense period, Eisenhower kept his foreign policy staff busy attempting to negotiate an end to the military adventure. As a direct result of Eisenhower's efforts, British and French power in the Middle East was finally broken, and the United States was left as the only significant Western power with influence in the region.

Eisenhower's fourth foreign policy crisis was by far the most damaging and embarrassing to both the country and indeed to Eisenhower himself. In 1960 Soviet forces shot down an American U-2 "Blackbird" spy plane over Soviet territory and captured the pilot, Francis Gary Powers. Eisenhower, who had stated many times that the United States was not flying spy missions over the Soviet Union, believed that Powers had been killed, and again made a national address in which he announced that the United States was not spying on the Soviets. With masterful aplomb, Soviet premier Nikita Khrushchev then produced Powers and demanded an explanation from the United States. Eisenhower, who had been clearly caught lying to both the American public and to the entire world, responded angrily, refusing to expand upon his earlier statement. While the United States and the Soviet Union had been moving toward a period of growing understanding and cooperation, the U-2 incident soured relations considerably and set the stage for a dramatic showdown between Khrushchev and Eisenhower's successor, John F. Kennedy.

Eisenhower's Legacy

Immediately after Eisenhower left office, many critics denounced his two terms as unproductive and lethargic. In later years, however, historians and political scientists have sought to demonstrate that underneath Eisenhower's seemingly laid-back exterior the president was fully and completely in control of national and international affairs. His presidency, writes historian Herbert S. Parmet, "came to be seen later as an artful example of holding the line against political and social forces . . . the leadership that seemed timid and uncreative at the time was later described by historians as adroit management of a not-so-placid decade."[14]

Ultimately, history's final judgment of Eisenhower may rest more upon his character than upon his policies. Many of those who have held the office of president have served more for their own glory than for the well-being of the nation. Dwight David Eisenhower was not that sort of man. Eisenhower made mistakes and supported positions that may have been inappropriate, but even when he was speaking against school desegregation or failing to take action on a significant civil rights question, Eisenhower was attempting to do what he thought was best for the country. Eisenhower felt that it was his duty to hold the office of the presidency above himself, and as president he unflinchingly sought to do that duty by upholding the law and—always—protecting the United States of America.

Notes

1. Dwight David Eisenhower, speech to the Canadian Club, Ottawa, Canada, January 10, 1945.
2. Eisenhower, address to the nation on the Farm Bill veto, April 16, 1956.
3. Eisenhower, orders to proceed with the Normandy invasion, at a conference of Allied military leaders in England, June 5, 1944.
4. Eisenhower, note prepared in case of failure on D day, June 6,

1944. The note is archived at the Eisenhower Center in Abilene, Kansas.

5. Eisenhower, campaign speeches, 1952.
6. Eisenhower, campaign speeches, 1952.
7. President Woodrow Wilson to the U.S. Congress, August 1914.
8. Senator Joseph McCarthy, speech to the Women's Republican Club of Wheeling, West Virginia, February 9, 1950.
9. McCarthy, speech to the Women's Republican Club in Wheeling, West Virginia, February 9, 1950.
10. Joseph Welch to Senator Joseph McCarthy, Army-McCarthy hearings, June 9, 1954.
11. Quoted in James T. Patterson, *Brown v. Board of Education: A Civil Rights Milestone and Its Troubled Legacy.* New York: Oxford University Press, 2001, p. 23.
12. Eisenhower, address to the nation on sending troops into Little Rock, September 24, 1957.
13. Eisenhower, campaign speech, October 24, 1952.
14. Herbert S. Parmet, "Eisenhower" in Eric Foner and John A. Garraty, eds., *The Reader's Companion to American History.* Boston: Houghton Mifflin, 1991, p. 330.

CHAPTER
1

CONTAINING
COMMUNISM

Limitations of the New Look

Walter LaFeber

The Eisenhower administration termed its approach to foreign policy the "New Look," and based it on the threat of "massive retaliation" to Soviet aggression. However, the New Look was designed to counter the Soviet Union itself, not the many smaller Communist regimes that sprang up during the 1950s. Ironically, because the United States was so powerful and could threaten total and complete nuclear destruction of any country that defied its will, Eisenhower sacrificed flexibility and the ability to influence events on a small scale. In this excerpt from *America, Russia, and the Cold War, 1945–1996*, author Walter LaFeber describes how the New Look proved too unwieldy and inflexible. Eisenhower's problem, LaFeber argues, was that he was only willing to apply the doctrine of "massive retaliation" under clear-cut circumstances, and that left him unable to cope with the "gray areas" of world affairs. LaFeber is a professor of American history at Cornell University. His books include *The American Age: United States Foreign Policy at Home and Abroad Since 1750* and *The United States in Central America*.

FROM THE DECLARATION OF INDEPENDENCE UNTIL THE Civil War, Americans generally sympathized with revolutions abroad. In several respects, however, they dispensed their sympathy with care. They disliked revolutions

Excerpted from *America, Russia, and the Cold War, 1945–1996, Eighth Edition*, by Walter LaFeber (New York: The McGraw-Hill Companies, Inc., 1997). Copyright © 1997 by The McGraw-Hill Companies, Inc. Reprinted with permission.

that went beyond the political, social, and economic boundaries of their own. Americans also believed their own revolution superior to revolutions on the "right" (as [former President] John Quincy Adams viewed the Latin American upheavals) or on the "left." They best liked revolts on the North American continent, such as those in Florida, Texas, California, and Canada, which opened possible areas for annexation to the expanding Union.

In the middle of the nineteenth century, two events began to reshape American views toward revolutions: the continental conquest was completed, and Americans began emphasizing the commercial aspects of their foreign policy instead of landed expansion. These overseas commercial interests became especially important, for stability, peace, and confidence in the sanctity of contract were essential to any great trading venture. By 1900 the United States had burgeoned into a power which combined the interesting characteristics of being conservative ideologically and expansive economically. Such a combination would not be encouraging to revolution. Interventions against rebellions in Cuba and the Philippines were followed by Theodore Roosevelt's pronouncement that the United States would act as a policeman to prevent upheavals in the Caribbean area. A decade later Woodrow Wilson rationalized the use of economic and military force against Mexico with an ideological justification that employed the traditional American liberal rhetoric. The threat of revolution reached a crisis when, in 1917, Lenin joined the use of force to a doctrine worldwide in its ambitions and repugnant to most Americans.

The Eisenhower administration inherited this significant historical legacy. It became an heir to opposing revolutions at the point when European colonial rule and conservative monarchies crumbled before nationalist uprisings in the Middle East, Africa, Asia, and Latin America. The new spirit was captured by the highly corrupt King Farouk of Egypt. As nationalist army officers threw him out of Egypt, Farouk predicted that in a decade there would only "be five kings left: Hearts, Clubs, Diamonds, Spades, and England." He was not far wrong.

Eisenhower and [Secretary of State John Foster] Dulles understood and sympathized with much of the new nationalism. Their own people, after all, had won the first modern anticolonial struggle in 1776. Both men realized, moreover, that the worn-out British and French empires were breathing their last. They wanted the colonials quickly out of the way. When colonials remained, revolutionaries tended to move leftward in order to continue the struggle. Eisenhower preferred to attack that problem at the root by pushing out the Europeans. But Americans seldom seemed able to move fast enough. Revolutionaries in Iran, Indochina, and Guatemala gained ground. The President determined to stop them with force if necessary.

The problem thus became what kind of force Americans should use to control revolutions abroad. Eisenhower and Dulles, and indeed later all Americans, found themselves in a terrible bind. They did not want to fight conventional ground wars in Asia and Africa. Korea had vividly proved the dangers of such involvements. Using covert weapons employed by the Central Intelligence Agency could work in certain instances (and Eisenhower proved to be exceedingly skillful in employing the CIA), but in other cases the revolutionaries had gathered too much strength to be beaten by James Bond-like operations. Sometimes they even enjoyed direct Soviet or Chinese assistance.

Eisenhower's Foreign Policy Tactics

Eisenhower devised a package of tactics for dealing with unwanted revolutionaries. First, he turned loose the CIA in such places as Iran and Guatemala, which were not yet out of control. Second, he sent U.S. military advisers to train native troops, as in Vietnam, where Eisenhower began the so-called Vietnamization of the war against the communists a generation before "Vietnamization" became a catchword of Richard Nixon's policy in the early 1970s. Third, Eisenhower and Dulles engineered a series of military alliances to tie friends together in a common fight against the Soviets outside, and left-wing revolutionaries inside, various regions. The Baghdad Pact in the Middle East and the Southeast Asia Treaty Organization (SEATO) became two of the more famous examples of "pactomania," as Dulles's critics labeled the policy. Fourth, Eisenhower based his overall military policy on the use of huge hydrogen bombs as well as small tactical atomic weapons that planners believed could be deployed with almost surgical precision on battlefields. He especially threatened to use these weapons if Soviet or Chinese forces launched a direct invasion or became heavily involved with the revolutionaries (as, indeed, he had already threatened in Korea in mid-1953).

The President's growing reliance on nuclear bombs also grew out of his determination to cut back government spending. No President in the post-1945 years has been as fanatic in this regard as this famous military commander who dedicated himself to slashing military budgets. He preached repeatedly that the key to American power was its economic system and marvelous productivity, not its weapons. Military spending on the level of Truman's $50 billion annually, he feared, would set off a terrible inflation and ruin the economy. "We must not go broke," he reiterated. To Eisenhower, "broke" meant either a deficit in the federal budget, or an economy growing dependent on a "military-industrial complex," as he later termed it. "To Eisenhower," a close observer later remarked, "the United States economy was like the source of a mother's milk— tender and soft and not to be abused."

At the same time, however, the President set out to stop left-wing revolutions and continue Truman's "containment" policy. These conclusions had been hammered out in a series of discussions during 1953 in "Operation Solarium" (named after the White House sun room in which they were held). If Eisenhower hoped to carry cut Truman's policies without Truman's budget, his only solution was to rely on nuclear weapons that were cheaper than maintaining men in arms in a conventional force. In two years Eisenhower reduced Truman's military budget by nearly one-third to about $34 billion. His reliance on nuclear armaments to accomplish this reduction soon became evident as he allowed the development of the B-41 bomb of over 20 megatons, or the equivalent of 400 Hiroshima-type bombs. (The B-41 proved less usable than originally anticipated after tests revealed that if it were dropped close to Soviet coastlines, the radiation would pose greater dangers to U.S. forces and ships at sea than it would to large parts of Russia itself.) The size of the nation's nuclear stockpile doubled between 1953 and 1955, while new, huge B-52 bombers rolled off assembly lines to deliver the weapons. Eisenhower became the first President to consider atomic and nuclear bombs "conventional" weapons—to "be used exactly as you would use a bullet or anything else," as he remarked publicly in 1955. Eisenhower refused repeatedly to accept a nuclear test ban that would have stopped the deadly radioactive fallout from weapons tests that began to infect the world's food supplies. His refusal was based in part on the Soviets' refusal to agree to what he considered adequate inspections, in part on the belief that the development of his main weapons systems depended on such tests. Thus, Eisenhower was prepared to consider starting a nuclear war if necessary— not only if the Soviets invaded Europe but also if Cold War costs became so high that they were forcing "us to war—or into some form of dictatorial government."

His strategy became known as "the new look," or "more bang for a buck." Dulles used the phrase "massive retaliation," by which he meant being "willing and able to respond vigorously at places and with means of [our] own choosing." Eisenhower had a clear sense of when he might launch "massive retaliation," as noted above. But he also had an idea of the destruction that could result. In certain situations, no matter how tempting, war had to be avoided. For example, he made a remarkable response to Syngman Rhee in mid-1954 when the South Korean leader tried to shame him into supporting a war to unify Korea. Eisenhower interrupted to say that he "regretted very much" the division of Korea, Germany, Austria, and Vietnam, "but . . . no one in this world will get America to go to war over these problems. . . . We cannot undertake any engagement that involves [the] deliberate intention of going to war with Iron Curtain countries."

Unable to Handle the "Gray Areas"

Eisenhower thereby defined the two extremes in which he would or would not go to war. But the extremes turned out not to be the problems. His dilemma involved the "gray areas"—as a young Harvard professor, Henry Kissinger, called them in 1955—the newly emerging areas where kings and colonials were giving way to nationalist revolutionary movements. In these areas Eisenhower faced the great challenge that has confronted all his successors: finding a way of successfully using U.S. power and—most important—understanding these movements. His first challenges arose in Iran, Guatemala, and Vietnam. The nation's response to these challenges was historic for it demonstrated the irrelevance of "massive retaliation" and unfortunately locked into place American beliefs about handling revolutionaries for the next twenty years.

The Mixed Success of "Massive Retaliation"

Robert F. Burk

When Eisenhower entered office he was faced with the specter of an expanding Soviet Union that was aggressively supporting the growth of communism throughout the Third World. He also faced demands from the right wing of the Republican Party to reduce government spending. In response, Eisenhower developed the New Look, under which he worked to decrease the size of the U.S. armed forces while increasing the number of nuclear weapons in the U.S. arsenal. Any threat to the United States or its allies, Eisenhower announced, would be met by "massive retaliation" and nuclear holocaust.

In this excerpt from *Dwight D. Eisenhower: Hero and Politician*, Robert F. Burk argues that Eisenhower was forced to institute the New Look because of partisan political pressures. Burk also maintains that the effectiveness of the threat of "massive retaliation" was decidedly mixed: By holding forth the specter of nuclear holocaust, Eisenhower was able to bring the Korean conflict to an end, prevent Communist China from seizing Taiwanese territory, and effectively halt serious Communist territorial expansion. At the same time, however, Eisenhower's obvious hesitance to actually deploy nuclear weapons resulted in his being unable to roll back communism where it had already made inroads. Burk is a history professor at Muskingum College in Ohio and the author of several books on U.S. history, including *The Eisenhower Administration and Black Civil Rights*.

W HEN DWIGHT EISENHOWER ENTERED THE WHITE House in January of 1953, he believed his primary responsibility was to promote and maintain American national security. By outlook, training, and personal preference, he intended first and foremost to be a foreign policy president. To that task he brought various assumptions about the postwar world and the American role in it. With the depression and World War II as his frame of reference, he saw the promotion of American prosperity and power around the world and the halt of the spread of totalitarianism as essential and complementary goals. To him the communist threat was real and was centrally directed from Moscow. Third World countries were dominoes in a gigantic big-power game, and Western economic and military security depended on preventing the Soviets from triggering the fall of these national dominoes through either overt aggression or internal revolutionary subversion. Third World nationalism was genuine, but it inevitably had to swing to one big-power pole or another. Like Truman, he posited a stable, supportive Western Europe as the chief anchor of American global security, and despite his earlier campaign rhetoric, he did not share the Asia-first orientation of the Republican Old Guard.

In his view, the nature of the communist enemy was such that, although American policy had to be based upon moral ends, America had to play by the same amoral rules as the opponent. Wars, whether hot or cold, required a cold-blooded calculus of strategy and tactics. As befitted the bridge-playing Eisenhower, the cold war was an analytical, almost mathematical, sequence of global responses and counterresponses. And like a good cardplayer, he kept his decision-making processes and his geopolitical tactics secret except when public diplomacy itself proved useful for public relations purposes or as bluff. As Vice-President Nixon described it, "He always applied two, three, or four lines of reasoning to a single problem and he usually preferred the indirect approach where it would serve him better than the direct attack on the problem."

Eisenhower in Command

Despite the attention paid to the public fulminations of Secretary of State John Foster Dulles, Eisenhower was in firm control of foreign policy in his administration. His preferred agency for crucial decisions was not the cabinet, but the National Security Council (NSC) and its smaller informal subgroups. Although the NSC had been created in 1947, President Truman had seldom used it. Eisenhower, seeking a more orderly, secretive body for foreign policy advice which would be comparable to a military staff, quickly revitalized it. The NSC's chief note taker and organizer was Robert Cutler, who as special assistant for national security affairs expanded its membership to include the secretary of the treasury and the budget director as well as others on an occasional basis. The major players at the table, however, were Eisenhower himself, the secretaries of state and defense, the chairman of the Joint Chiefs of Staff, and the director of the Central Intelligence Agency. Eisenhower held NSC meetings weekly, prefaced by briefings from CIA Director Allen Dulles, the secretary of state's brother. Despite his numerous serious illnesses during his presidency, Eisenhower missed only twenty-nine meetings of the NSC in eight years. "Its sessions are long, bitter, and tough," he noted. "Out of that sort of discussion we're trying to hammer policy."

What the public saw for the majority of the Eisenhower years was the deceptive sight of Secretary of State Dulles issuing moral lectures on the evils of communism and delivering calls for the "liberation" of Eastern Europe. Dulles, the long-time Republican party spokesman on foreign policy, had been selected by Eisenhower partly to satisfy the Old Guard. Although Eisenhower respected Dulles's intelligence and the secretary's advice often intrigued him, he by no means always followed it. Dulles proved most useful as a lightning rod for criticism—an official whose visible position enabled him to provide rhetorical bluster at communist rivals when necessary. Dulles also helped Eisenhower convince Americans that he was sincere in seeking to free the "captive nations" of Eastern Europe, although no practical ways to achieve that aim existed.

With hindsight it is easier to see that Eisenhower's approach to foreign policy was dictated in large measure by the contradictory partisan pressures operating upon him. [Since] 1948, Republicans had hammered away at the Democrats for adopting a containment policy that they claimed was too "passive," instead of attempting to "roll back" communist gains. At the same time, the Republicans had condemned their partisan opponents for preempting congressional authority while spending too much money and bankrupting the country. Defense spending, however, made up a large share of the increase in the federal budget. How, then, could Eisenhower bolster American alliances in Europe, offer at least lip service to the strident calls for liberation, and reduce American defense expenditures at the same time? . . .

The "New Look" and "Massive Retaliation"

Eisenhower's defense-policy answer to the strident calls from the Republican Right for both fiscal restraint and militant anticommunism came packaged in two phrases— the "New Look" and "massive retaliation." The New Look, formulated in NSC sessions in the fall and winter of 1953, promised a cutback in conventional forces from twenty divisions to fourteen by 1957, and the navy would absorb lesser cuts. But the air force, acquiring thirty thousand more men, would be increased from 115 to 137 wings. Ground forces stationed overseas would be reduced, but in order to preserve sufficient deterrent power against the Soviets and their allies the threat of massive retaliation would become official American defense doctrine. Smaller tactical nuclear weapons would be used in local wars, but the main American retaliatory response around the globe now would be the unpredictable application of massive nuclear force directly against the Soviet Union or China. The intended result would be, in the parlance of the day, "more bang for the buck." By relying to an unprecedented extent upon the air force, the defense budget then could be reduced from \$35 billion to \$31 billion a year.

Such, at least, was the official strategy, designed as much to pacify conservative Republicans as to humble the Russians and their allies. Unfortunately, the New Look's reliance on massive retaliation did not work except as a strategy of bluff. If the enemy was willing to believe in the American threat of nuclear reprisal, bluff could force diplomatic gains. But the more often massive retaliation was used as threat and not as reality, it would tend to lose its power to intimidate the adversary into concessions. The New Look approach did not mesh with the parallel objective of improved defense cooperation with Western Europe. When crises arose and the United States sought alliance sanction for its use of massive retaliatory response, the European allies resisted joining in, fearing a Soviet counterresponse and the condemnation of world opinion. Eisenhower himself proved consistently unwilling to provoke international opinion by ordering retaliatory action without the protective umbrella of Allied joint participation. Western Europe also opposed any American schemes to increase European levels of military spending and troop strength so that the United States could reduce its own. As a consequence, the New Look's chief accomplishments proved not to be its military and diplomatic results but its contributions to defusing the Republican Right and to temporarily holding down American military spending.

During the Eisenhower years, the massive retaliation doctrine did nothing to halt the Soviets' consolidation of their hold on Eastern Europe. The hollowness of the American threats of massive response and liberation were demonstrated as early as June 1953, when riots broke out in Soviet-occupied East Berlin and spread to other cities. Within twenty-four hours Soviet tanks had brutally crushed the resistance. The only official American response was to open food kitchens in West Berlin for the influx of refugees. Similarly in 1956, bold American words were not followed by bold actions. Following a modest loosening of Soviet policy in Poland that had permitted the installation of moderate Wladyslaw Gomulka as head of the Polish Communist party on 21 October 1956, rioting broke out in Hungary. Rebels demanded a similar relaxation of Russian control and specifically the return of Imre Nagy as Hungarian premier. At first the Russians showed restraint, allowing Nagy's return and pulling Soviet tanks out of Budapest. But while the CIA-funded Radio Free Europe broadcast militant calls to arms into Hungary, all Eisenhower could offer was the comment to a journalist after a campaign stop, "Poor fellows, poor fellows, I think about them all the time. I wish there were some way of helping them." After Nagy announced his intention to pull Hungary out of the Warsaw Pact, the Russians retook the country by force. Thirty thousand Hungarians were killed, 200,000 fled the country as refugees, and Nagy was executed by a Soviet firing squad in 1958. . . .

A Dangerous Showdown

The continuing danger that America's use of brinksmanship could lead to an irreversible big-power showdown and a nuclear exchange was dramatically underscored during yet another series of crises in the Far East. This time the confrontation pitted Chaing Kai-Shek's Nationalist Chinese, exiled on the island of Formosa, against the mainland Communists. The focus of the dispute was each side's claim to a series of offshore islands, particularly Quemoy and Matsu. Chiang's forces held the islands, as potential stepping-stones to the mainland, with seventy-five thousand Nationalist troops, while Mao Tse-tung's government claimed them as its rightful property. The first Quemoy crisis had erupted in September 1954, when Communist shelling of the island had killed two American soldiers. Eisenhower had rejected a . . . recommendation to bomb the Chinese mainland, but he had given Chiang an agreement promising U.S. protection of Formosa and "such other territories as may be determined by mutual agreement" in exchange for his agreement to a cease-fire. After a brief cooling-off period, however, Communist shelling had resumed against the Nationalist-held Tachen Islands two hundred miles north of Formosa. In response, Eisenhower strengthened his guarantee with Chiang to include defense of Quemoy and Matsu if he agreed to evacuate the Tachens. In early March 1955, Secretary Dulles coupled Eisenhower's communications to Chiang with vague threats of atomic reprisal against the mainland if the Communists persisted in their aggression in the Taiwan Straits.

The result of Eisenhower's parallel guarantees and threats in the region was a war scare in Washington and Peking, and the initiation of direct discussions between the United States and Communist China in Geneva in August. The shelling of the Nationalist-held islands again stopped temporarily, but the basic issue of the islands' ownership remained unresolved. Not surprisingly, in August 1958, the crisis exploded again, following additional troop buildups on Quemoy by Chiang. In response the Communists attempted, this time through both shelling and a naval blockade, to cut off Nationalist supplies to the island. Again the Eisenhower administration employed the tacit threat of massive response and positioned the Seventh

Fleet for a possible attack on the Communist blockade. In the background briefing to reporters, Dulles let it be known that the United States now considered an attack on Quemoy or Matsu as an attack on Formosa itself, which would require a full American military response.

Both Sides Back Away

This time, however, official administration statements did not bring forward a Communist withdrawal but instead counterthreats from the Soviet Union. On 7 September 1958, Nikita Khrushchev bluntly warned Eisenhower that "an attack on the Chinese People's Republic is an attack on the Soviet Union." Both sides, staring down the precipice of nuclear war, proceeded to back away from a showdown. Negotiations resumed between the Communist Chinese and the Americans, and although the administration stood by its defense commitment to Chiang, it noticeably cooled its rhetoric. The Communists, in turn, effectively ended their blockade's utility by announcing to the world their intention to scale back shelling of Quemoy to a token, every-other-day schedule. Bemused at this unusual approach to defusing a crisis, Eisenhower remarked, "I wondered if we were in a Gilbert and Sullivan war." Observers were left to speculate on the consequences, however, had both sides stood fast rather than compromised. Privately Eisenhower sought to reassure nervous Allies that he had not intended to use "even tactical atomic weapons in a limited operation." But was even such a use of nuclear bluff wise or necessary in resolving the fate of several offshore islands in the Taiwan Straits?

In the long run, what controversies like that over Quemoy and Matsu demonstrated was that in a world on which two opposing superpowers possessed nuclear arsenals, talking out differences and seeking a basis of accommodation made more sense than games of nuclear blackmail. Despite his skill at the nuclear chess game, Eisenhower himself regularly acknowledged the need for improved relations with the Soviets, as long as such conciliation did not compromise American objectives. But an atmosphere colored by brinksmanship and cold war rhetoric made superpower agreement on nuclear arms control and other outstanding issues virtually impossible. . . .

Short-Term Successes, Long-Term Drawbacks

By the end of the Eisenhower presidency, a decided gap had formed between the short-term successes of his foreign policy and its longer term drawbacks. Through the New Look, Eisenhower had exerted a successful temporary restraint upon the fiscal hunger of the "military-industrial complex." His unwillingness to undertake open unilateral military intervention in Vietnam in 1954 had postponed, at least, the commitment of American ground forces to the South. His strategy of nuclear bluff apparently had hastened the resolution of the Korean War, and his willingness to show restraint in the employment of force had prevented the triggering of atomic war over Quemoy and Matsu. Although lacking a formal agreement, he nonetheless had secured an informal pause in the atmospheric testing of nuclear weapons. But he had not rolled back communism where it already existed, and the rhetoric of liberation had not offered him any more clout to do so than had the doctrine of containment for Truman. No mutual basis for long-term coexistence between the United States and the Soviet Union had been found, and in its absence the race to develop superior intercontinental ballistic missiles continued and threatened to accelerate. In the Third World, perceived threats to American economic security and to global stability had been met through covert action, but at the cost of casting America as the new defender of Western colonial imperialism and political repression. A strange new world of emerging nations and complex economic and political arrangements was surfacing to challenge the old verities of a bipolar worldview. But recognition of the new realities, and the new limits they imposed on American power, would have to await subsequent presidents and their own foreign policy teams.

Eisenhower's Handling of the Suez Crisis

Robert A. Divine

The Egyptian seizure and closure of the Suez Canal on July 26, 1956, was an event of critical importance during the Eisenhower presidency. The Suez Canal provides access from the Mediterranean Sea to the oilfields of the Middle East, and so Egypt's actions threatened the world's oil supply. Britain and France, up until that time the two most influential Western powers involved in Middle Eastern politics, entered a secret agreement with Israel intended to result in international control of the canal. Under this agreement, the Israelis would attack the Suez Canal area, thus "forcing" France and England to demand that both Egypt and Israel withdraw entirely. Eisenhower was furious when he learned about the agreement—after the Israeli attack—and worked to prevent both a global war and increased Soviet domination of the vital Middle East.

In this excerpt from *Eisenhower and the Cold War*, Robert A. Divine argues that Eisenhower's refusal to aid the British and the French and his insistence that Israel withdraw from captured territory resulted in the United States supplanting Europe as the most important outside influence in the Middle East. Divine was for many years a professor of history at the University of Texas in Austin, and he is the author of numerous books on U.S. diplomatic and foreign policy history, including *Roosevelt and World War II* and *The Sputnik Challenge*.

Excerpted from *Eisenhower and the Cold War*, by Robert A. Divine (New York: Oxford University Press, 1981). Copyright © 1981 by Robert A. Divine. Reprinted by permission of Oxford University Press.

THE EGYPTIAN SEIZURE OF THE SUEZ CANAL ON JULY 26, 1956, presented Eisenhower with the most severe crisis of his entire presidency. For the next four months, as the 1956 election campaign ran its course, the President attempted to restrain England and France, and when these efforts failed, he applied economic and political pressure to secure a peaceful resolution of the Suez crisis. In the process, the Western alliance suffered severe strains, but Eisenhower achieved his major goals—preventing a global war and blocking Soviet domination of the vital Middle East.

In the months that followed the cease-fire on November 7, 1956, President Eisenhower sought to restore order in the Middle East. His policy had two clear goals. The first was short-range and manageable—persuade the British, French, and Israelis to withdraw from the Egyptian territory they had seized. The second was long-range and less easily attained—prevent the Soviets from exploiting the British and French defeat to expand their influence in the Middle East. Eisenhower's pursuit of these two goals required a new and vigorous American policy in an area previously considered a preserve of our European allies.

The Military Situation at Suez

The situation following the cease-fire was very confused. Israel was in good shape, with its forces in control of the Gaza Strip and Sharm el-Sheikh; the British and French were in an awkward position, controlling Port Said at the north end of the canal, which Nasser had blocked with forty scuttled ships when the fighting began. The United Nations was preparing to send in an emergency force to occupy the canal area and permit the evacuation of the European troops. Meanwhile, the canal closure, coupled with the sabotage of the main pipeline from the Persian Gulf to the Mediterranean, had created a serious oil shortage in Western Europe. England and France normally relied on the Middle East for 75 per cent of their petroleum; unless they received emergency shipments from the United States, they would soon run out of gasoline for their cars, heat for their homes, and energy for their factories.

The Eisenhower administration decided to take advantage of this oil crunch. Although the President at first had wanted to invite [British Prime Minister Anthony Robert] Eden to Washington for a conference, State Department officials finally persuaded him to hew to a hard line. The United States, the President declared, could offer no assistance to England and France until they withdrew their troops from the canal area. Instead of convening the Middle East Emergency Committee to arrange for the transfer of Western Hemisphere oil to Europe, Eisenhower deliberately suspended this government-industry effort, despite protests from American oil companies. A dismayed Anthony Eden admitted that he had not foreseen that "The United States Government would harden against us on almost every point and become harsher after the cease-fire than before." Deprived of petroleum, England and France had no choice but to give in. Assured that the requested evacuation would take place soon, the President on November 30 authorized the beginning of an oil lift to Western Europe whereby fifteen American companies arranged for the shipment of 500,000 barrels of oil a day, partly from increased American and Venezuelan production, partly from a diversion of Persian Gulf oil. Three days later, the British announced that they would remove their troops from Egypt, and on December 22 the last English and French units left the canal area, thus ending the disastrous Suez expedition.

The USSR and the Eisenhower Doctrine

The President was deeply concerned with the possibility of Soviet advance into the area as the British and French left. He conferred with a recuperating [Secretary of State] John Foster Dulles on this problem in December, and then he and the secretary shared their conclusions with a small group of congressional leaders at a New Year's Day meeting at the White House. "The existing vacuum in the Middle East," Eisenhower declared, "must be filled by the United States before it is filled by Russia." He went on to explain that he planned to ask Congress for a special economic fund to aid Arab nations threatened by communism and for authority to use force to repel Soviet aggression. The congressmen and senators were dubious about the new commitment, expressing reservations over the use of force. The President assured them he would not act without specific congressional approval and only on the request of a Middle Eastern country, adding that if the authority were granted, "it might never have to be used." Eisenhower conceded that he had the power to act on his own in an emergency, but he wanted Congress to help him "make our intent clear in advance."

The President submitted his formal request to Congress in a special message on January 5, 1957. "Russia's rulers have long sought to dominate the Middle East," he began. "This was true of the Czars and it is true of the Bolsheviks. . . ." Then he laid out what soon became known as the Eisenhower Doctrine, a three-part grant of authority for presidential action in the Middle East. First, he asked for $200 million in economic assistance to preserve the independence of "any nation or group of nations in the general area of the Middle East"; second, he requested military assistance for the same countries; finally, he called on Congress to permit him to use the armed forces to protect Middle Eastern nations "requesting such aid" against "overt armed aggression from any nation controlled by International Communism."

Critics quickly pointed out the weaknesses in the Eisenhower Doctrine. Soviet penetration was most likely in Egypt and Syria, nations unlikely to request aid from the United States. The main threat to the independence of pro-Western countries, such as Jordan and Lebanon, came from the rising strength of Arab nationalism, personified by Nasser, and not from "International Communism." Most Arab spokesmen warned the United States to stay out of the Middle East, vowing that they could solve their problems without American help. Even at home, there was doubt, with Dean Acheson dismissing the Eisenhower Doctrine as "vague, inadequate and not very helpful."

Despite this reaction, the President did not waver. In a letter to Churchill in November 1956, Eisenhower had expressed the sorrow he felt over opposing Britain on Suez, and then had added, "The Soviets are the real enemy of the Western World, implacably hostile and seeking our de-

The Eisenhower Doctrine

The United States through the joint action of the President and the Congress, or, in the case of treaties, the Senate, has manifested in many endangered areas its purpose to support free and independent governments—and peace—against external menace, notably the menace of International Communism. Thereby we have helped to maintain peace and security during a period of great danger. It is now essential that the United States should manifest through joint action of the President and the Congress our determination to assist those nations of the Mid East area, which desire that assistance.

The action which I propose would have the following features:

It would, first of all, authorize the United States to cooperate with and assist any nation or group of nations in the general area of the Middle East in the development of economic strength dedicated to the maintenance of national independence.

It would, in the second place, authorize the Executive to undertake in the same region programs of military assis-

struction." He firmly believed that they "had their eyes on the Middle East," and that if the United States did not stand squarely in Russia's path, communism would sweep over the entire area. In particular, the President worried about Soviet designs on Persian Gulf oil, claiming that they did not need this precious resource for themselves but rather planned "to seize the oil, to cut the canal and the pipelines of the Middle East, and thus seriously to weaken Western civilization." Eisenhower was apparently convinced that it was an American obligation to block "the Soviet Union's march . . . to the underground lakes of oil which fuel the homes and factories of Western Europe." Having just ex-

tance and cooperation with any nation or group of nations which desires such aid.

It would, in the third place, authorize such assistance and cooperation to include the employment of the armed forces of the United States to secure and protect the territorial integrity and political independence of such nations, requesting such aid, against overt armed aggression from any nation controlled by International Communism.

These measures would have to be consonant with the treaty obligations of the United States, including the Charter of the United Nations and with any action or recommendations of the United Nations. They would also, if armed attack occurs, be subject to the overriding authority of the United Nations Security Council in accordance with the Charter.

The present proposal would, in the fourth place, authorize the President to employ, for economic and defensive military purposes, sums available under the Mutual Security Act of 1954, as amended, without regard to existing limitations.

Dwight D. Eisenhower, Special Message to Congress on the Situation in the Middle East, January 5, 1957.

ploited this vulnerability to effect British and French withdrawal from Suez, the President was especially sensitive to the importance of petroleum to the world economy.

The Senate Withholds Support

Congress did not share Eisenhower's sense of urgency over the Middle East resolution. The House acted promptly, voting 355 to 61 for the authority which the President had requested. But in the Senate doubts about extending aid to Arab nations troubled supporters of Israel, while the Democratic leadership, still smarting from Eisenhower's re-election, insisted on modifying the administration's resolution. Senator Lyndon Johnson was successful in amending the legislation to deny a specific authorization for the use of troops; instead, the Senate simply stated that the United States "is prepared" to employ force if the President "determines the necessity thereof."

Despite Dulles's objection, the President had agreed to the new wording when a new problem in the Middle East postponed further action on the Eisenhower Doctrine. The Israelis had withdrawn their troops from most of the Sinai in November, but they continued to hold two key areas—the Gaza Strip and Sharm el-Sheikh. In February 1957, Prime Minister David Ben Gurion declared that Israel would insist on maintaining police power in Gaza to prevent a recurrence of Arab terrorist raids and on retaining the strategic post that controlled access to the Gulf of Aqaba and the port of Elath. Egypt refused to reopen the Suez Canal while Israel occupied portions of the Sinai, thereby intensifying the continued oil shortage in Western Europe, which had been only partially alleviated by the American oil lift. A worried Eisenhower, declaring that "We must not allow Europe to go flat on its back for the want of oil," decided now to back UN efforts to apply economic sanctions against Israel to compel a full withdrawal from Gaza and Sharm el-Sheikh. Senate Majority Leader Lyndon

Johnson, however, immediately raised an objection to American pressure against Israel. In a letter to Dulles, Johnson asked the secretary to instruct the American delegation to the United Nations to oppose "with all its skill" any attempt to impose sanctions on Israel. There clearly would be no further Senate action on the Eisenhower Doctrine until the threat against Israel was removed.

Eisenhower Feuds with Israel and the Senate

Dulles flew to Georgia, where the President was vacationing at Secretary of the Treasury George Humphrey's hunting lodge. Informed of the Senate objections, Eisenhower was insistent on applying economic pressure on Israel, even to the extent of cutting off private American assistance, estimated to run at over $100 million a year. Then he agreed to cut short his vacation and return to Washington for a showdown with the Senate leaders.

The resulting White House conference on February 20 was long and angry. The President tried to impress upon the congressional leaders the vital need to reopen the Suez Canal and resume the normal flow of oil. If the United States permitted Israel to retain territory it had conquered, Eisenhower warned, the result would be "increased influence of Russia in the Arab states," "interruption of the flow of oil," "possibly a serious crash in the French and United Kingdom economies and, finally, an increased possibility of general war." Neither Lyndon Johnson nor Senate Minority Leader William Knowland was impressed, and it soon became clear that the Senate would not cooperate in imposing sanctions against Israel. Eisenhower could not believe that domestic political considerations "could enter so much into life-or-death, peace-or-war decisions." He finally told the congressmen and senators that he would take the issue to the American people. House Speaker Sam Rayburn approved, commenting, "America has either one voice or none, and that voice is the voice of the President—

whether everybody agrees with him or not."

That evening the President spoke to the nation by radio and television. "The future of the United Nations and peace in the Middle East may be at stake," he began, and then proceeded to outline the Israeli refusal to withdraw and the United Nations plan for economic sanctions. "If we agree that armed attack can properly achieve the purposes of the assailant," Eisenhower declared, "then I fear we will have turned back the clock of international order." He then stated his belief that the United Nations had "no choice but to exert pressure upon Israel," and indicated that he would cooperate in this effort.

The Crisis Resolved

The President's firm stand finally convinced the Israelis. During the last week of February, several intermediaries, including French Foreign Minister Christian Pineau and Canadian Foreign Minister Lester Pearson, worked out a compromise whereby the United Nations Emergency Force would occupy both Gaza and Sharm el-Sheikh. President Eisenhower, in addition, reaffirmed an earlier American pledge to uphold "the right of free and innocent passage" of the Gulf of Aqaba and "to join with others to secure general recognition of this right." Accordingly, on March 1, 1957, Golda Meir, the Israeli foreign minister, informed the UN General Assembly of her nation's plans for a total withdrawal of troops from the disputed areas.

The logjam then broke quickly. On March 2, Senator Johnson defeated an amendment to eliminate references to economic and military assistance from the Eisenhower Doctrine; a week later, the Senate passed the resolution by the comfortable margin of 58 to 28. The last detachment of Israeli troops left the Sinai on March 6, surrendering their positions to the UN Emergency Force. Finally, the Suez Canal reopened on March 29 when a convoy of nine freighters made the first passage since October 1956. Once again oil flowed by tanker through the canal, thus relieving the intense fuel shortage in Western Europe. Best of all for the president, the Israeli withdrawal had ended the danger of a showdown between the executive and legislative branches over economic sanctions.

It is difficult to decide if anyone emerged victorious from the long and debilitating Suez crisis. Nasser became a hero in the Arab world, but his army had been soundly defeated by the Israelis and his country had met with serious economic reverses during the canal's closure. The Russians had undoubtedly increased their influence in the Middle East, but they had never shown the ambition attributed to them by Eisenhower and Dulles, and they were very cautious in the face of the prevailing Arab nationalism. Peter Lyon argues that the Eisenhower administration was the only "winner," since the United States had come out of the Suez fiasco as the "presumptive protector of the Middle East" and the guardian of the oil so vital to Western Europe. Certainly from this time forward, the United States would be the dominant Western influence in the area, and American companies would control an ever-greater portion of the Persian Gulf oil in the days before OPEC. Eisenhower had succeeded in his goal of filling the vacuum in the Middle East, replacing England and France there just as in 1954 he had supplanted the French in Indochina. Yet the price was also great—alienation of the nation's oldest and most reliable allies. There is great irony in the fact that Eisenhower, the man hailed as the savior of Western Europe in World War II, would become the president who extended American power and influence globally at the expense of England and France.

PRESIDENTS
and their
DECISIONS

CHAPTER
2

AVOIDING WAR IN VIETNAM

Bumbling or Brilliant?: Eisenhower's Decisions on U.S. Intervention in Vietnam

George C. Herring

In the spring of 1954 Eisenhower was faced with one of the most important foreign policy decisions of his administration: whether or not to support French forces at the Battle of Dien Bien Phu. France had long had a strong colonial presence in Vietnam, but the Communist-backed Viet Minh had been fighting Vietnamese independence for several years. In the valley of Dien Bien Phu, the French believed that they had lured the Viet Minh (led by General Vo Nguyen Giap) into a strategic ambush, but soon discovered that the Communist forces possessed overwhelming firepower and manpower. Desperate for assistance, French leaders requested that Eisenhower authorize air strikes against Viet Minh positions on the hills surrounding the French fortifications. After considering various military options, Eisenhower focused his attention on trying to organize an international coalition to pursue "United Action" in Southeast Asia. Ultimately, Eisenhower's efforts proved fruitless: Great Britain, the United States' most important ally, flatly refused to become involved in the French colonial conflict, and Eisenhower decided that the United States could not afford to become involved in a military conflict with France alone as a military ally.

In this excerpt from *America's Longest War: The United States*

Excerpted from *America's Longest War: The United States and Vietnam, 1950–1975*, by George C. Herring (New York: The McGraw-Hill Companies, Inc., 1996). Copyright © 1996 by The McGraw-Hill Companies, Inc. Reprinted with permission.

and Vietnam, 1950–1975, George C. Herring argues that it is difficult to assess Eisenhower's decisions about whether to intervene at Dien Bien Phu. In the end it is unclear whether or not Eisenhower wanted to intervene, and whether or not he pursued United Action in order to shift blame from himself for not ordering American air strikes. The historical record, points out Herring, supports both interpretations of Eisenhower's actions. Herring is a professor of history at the University of Kentucky and the author of numerous works including *The Secret Diplomacy of the Vietnam War: The Negotiating Volumes of the Pentagon Papers* and *LBJ and Vietnam: A Different Kind of War.*

[IN 1953] THE MILITARY AND POLITICAL SITUATION IN Indochina drastically deteriorated. . . . In the fall of 1953, [French General Henri Navarre] began mobilizing forces for the anticipated offensive in the [Red River] delta. Recognizing that he must strike a decisive blow before the impact of expanded American aid could be felt, [North Vietnamese General Vo Nguyen] Giap invaded central and southern Laos, intensified guerrilla activity in the delta, and prepared for a major strike into northern Laos. The only response Navarre could devise was to scatter the very forces he had just combined to counter the new Vietminh thrusts.

By early 1954, both sides had committed major forces to the remote village of Dienbienphu in the northwest corner of Vietnam.

Navarre established a position at the intersection of several major roads near the Laotian border to cut off the anticipated invasion and lure Vietminh main units into open battle. In a broad valley surrounded by hills as high as 1,000 feet, he constructed a garrison ringed with barbed wire and bunkers and hastily dispatched twelve battalions of regulars supported by aircraft and heavy artillery. Giap took the "bait." After a quick strike into Laos, he retraced his steps and encircled the French garrison. Navarre now found 12,000 of his elite forces isolated in a far corner of Vietnam. Although increasingly uncertain that they could hold out against superior Vietminh numbers, he decided to remain. . . .

Eisenhower Considers Intervention

In January 1954, the United States for the first time faced the prospect of direct military intervention in Indochina. Speaking with "great force," Eisenhower expressed to the National Security Council (NSC) bitter opposition to putting American troops into the jungles of Indochina. He went on to insist, however, that the United States could not forget its vital interests there. Comparing the region to a "leaky dike," he warned that it was "sometimes better to put a finger in than to let the whole structure wash away." American officials especially feared that French war-weariness would result in a surrender at [the 1954 peace talks in] Geneva [Switzerland]. A special committee reviewing Indochina policy recommended in mid-March that the United States should discourage defeatist tendencies in France and use its influence at Geneva to ensure that no agreements were reached. If, despite its efforts, the French accepted an unsatisfactory settlement, the United States might have to arrange with the Associated States [Vietnam, Laos, and Cambodia] and other interested nations to continue the war without France.

While Eisenhower and his advisers pondered U.S. intervention, Giap tightened the noose around Dienbienphu. On March 13, the Vietminh launched an all-out attack and within twenty-four hours had seized hills Gabrielle and Beatrice, the outposts established by France to protect the fortress in the valley below. American and French experts had predicted that it would be impossible to get artillery up to the high ground surrounding the garrison. But the Vietminh formed "human anthills," carrying disassembled weapons up piece by piece, then reassembling them and camouflaging them so effectively that they were impervious to artillery and strafing. The heavy Vietminh guns quickly knocked out the airfield, making resupply impossible except by parachute drop and leaving the garrison of 12,000 men isolated and vulnerable.

The spectacular Vietminh success at Dienbienphu raised the prospect of immediate U.S. intervention. During a visit to Washington in late March, the French chief of staff, General Paul Ely, still estimated a "50-50 chance of success" at Dienbienphu and merely requested the transfer of additional American aircraft to be used by France for attacks on Vietminh lines around the fortress. Ely was deeply concerned about the possibility of Chinese intervention, however, openly inquiring how the United States would respond in such a contingency. Much less optimistic about Dienbienphu, the JCS chairman, Admiral Arthur Radford, seized upon a scheme originally devised by French and American officers in Saigon. Code-named VULTURE, the plan in its various manifestations called for the bombing of Vietminh supply lines and entrenchments around Dienbienphu by U.S. B-29s, possibly unmarked or camouflaged with French markings and flown either by French crews, American military pilots, or U.S. military pilots temporarily assigned to the French Foreign Legion. Some discussion was given to the use of tactical nuclear weapons. Radford's enthusiasm for the plan led Ely to believe that U.S. approval would be forthcoming should the French formally request it. . . .

Air Strikes Opposed

Most of Eisenhower's top military advisers raised serious objections to air intervention at Dienbienphu. Some questioned whether an air strike could relieve the siege without destroying the fortress itself; others wondered whether intervention could be kept limited—"One cannot go over Niagara Falls in a barrel only slightly," a Defense Department analyst warned. Among the JCS, only Air Force General Nathan F. Twining approved the proposal, and he insisted on attaching conditions that the French were unlikely to accept. The other chiefs warned that air intervention posed major risks and would not decisively affect the outcome of the war. Army Chief of Staff Matthew Ridgway was particularly outspoken, responding to Radford's query about the proposed air strike with an "emphatic and immediate 'No.'" Alarmed by "the old delusive idea . . . that we could do things the cheap and easy way," Ridgway warned Eisenhower that air power alone could not ensure victory and that ground forces would have to fight under the most difficult logistic circumstances and in a uniquely inhospitable terrain.

Although profoundly skeptical about the proposed air strike at Dienbienphu, the administration was sufficiently alarmed by the emerging crisis in Indochina to seek congressional support for possible military intervention. The fall of Dienbienphu seemed certain by early April. Eisenhower and Dulles preferred to act in concert with other nations, but they feared that a defeat at Dienbienphu might produce a French collapse before plans for United Action could be put into effect, leaving American naval and air power the only means to save Indochina. Sensitive to Truman's fate in Korea, they were unwilling to act without backing from Congress, and Eisenhower instructed Dulles to explore with congressional leaders the conditions under which the use of American military power might be approved. The purpose of the dramatic meeting at the State Department on April 3 was not to secure approval for an immediate air attack but to gain discretionary authority to employ American naval and air forces—with allies if possible, without them if necessary—should the fall of Dienbienphu threaten the loss of Indochina.

The administration encountered stubborn resistance. Dulles and Radford grimly warned that failure to act might cost the United States Southeast Asia and advised that the President should have the power to use naval and air forces "if he felt it necessary in the interest of national security." No one questioned their assessment of the gravity of the situation, but the congressmen insisted that there must be "no more Koreas, with the United States furnishing 90% of the manpower," and made it clear that they would approve nothing until the administration had obtained firm commitments from other nations. Dulles persisted, assuring the legislators that the administration had no intention of sending ground troops to Indochina and indicating that he could more easily gain commitments from allies if he could specify what the United States would do. The congressmen were not swayed. "Once the flag is committed," they warned, "the use of land forces would surely follow." Sharing the administration's distrust of France, they also insisted that the United States must not go to war in support of colonialism. They would only agree that if "satisfactory commitments" could be secured from Great Britain and other allies to support military intervention, and from France to "internationalize" the war and speed the move toward independence, they would support a resolution authorizing the President to commit U.S. forces. Congressional insistence on prior allied commitments, particularly from Great Britain, eliminated the option of unilateral American intervention and placed major obstacles in the way of United Action. . . .

Call for United Action

With the fate of Dienbienphu hanging in the balance, the United States frantically promoted United Action. Dulles immediately departed for London and Paris to consult with British and French leaders. Eisenhower penned a long personal letter to Prime Minister Winston Churchill urging British support for a coalition that would be "willing to fight" to check Communist expansion in Southeast Asia. At a much publicized news conference on April 7, the President laid the foundation for possible U.S. intervention.

Outlining in simple language principles that had formed the basis for American policy for four years, he emphasized that Indochina was an important source of tin, tungsten, and rubber and that having lost China to "Communist dictatorship," the United States "simply can't afford greater losses." More important, he warned, should Indochina fall, the rest of Southeast Asia would "go over very quickly," like a "row of dominoes" when the first one is knocked down, causing much greater losses of raw materials and people, jeopardizing America's strategic position in the Far East, and driving Japan into the Communist camp. "So the possible consequences of the loss," he concluded, "are just incalculable to the free world."

The flurry of American diplomatic activity in April 1954 revealed fundamental cleavages between the United States and its allies. The Churchill government was prepared to join a collective security arrangement after Geneva, but it adamantly opposed immediate intervention in Indochina. Churchill and his foreign secretary, Anthony Eden, did not share the American fear that the loss of all or part of Indochina would bring the fall of Southeast Asia. They were convinced that France retained sufficient influence to salvage a reasonable settlement at Geneva, and they feared that outside military intervention would destroy any hope of a negotiated settlement and perhaps even provoke a war with China. Most important, they had no desire to entangle Britain in a war they were certain could not be won.

Dulles's discussions with France were equally unproductive and made clear the widely divergent approaches of the two nations toward the war and the Geneva negotiations. The United States was willing to intervene in Indochina, but only on condition that France resist a negotiated settlement at Geneva, agree to remain in Indochina and fight indefinitely, concede to its ally a greater role in planning strategy and training indigenous forces, and accept Vietnamese demands for complete independence. The

French insisted that Vietnam must retain ties with the French Union. They wanted nothing more than an air strike to relieve the siege of Dienbienphu. They opposed internationalization of the war, which would not only undermine their prestige in Indochina but also remove control from their hands. Dulles may have hoped that by offering to help France he could yet save the European Defense Community, but the French government made it clear that the EDC would have no chance of approval if France obligated itself to keep troops in Indochina indefinitely.

Tension Among Allies

The administration was deeply annoyed by the response of its allies. U.S. officials complained that the British were

---

The White House Dispatches an Ambassador to South Vietnam

"The President on November 3 designated Gen. J. Lawton Collins as Special United States Representative in Viet-Nam with the personal rank of Ambassador, to undertake a diplomatic mission of limited duration. He will coordinate the operations of all U.S. agencies in that country.

General Collins will proceed immediately to Saigon. . . . For the duration of this assignment General Collins will relinquish his other duties, including that of U.S. representative on the Military Committee of the North Atlantic Treaty Organization.

Since the conclusion of hostilities in Indochina, the U.S. Government has been particularly concerned over developments in Viet-Nam, a country ravaged by 8 years of war, artificially divided into armistice zones, and confronted by dangerous forces threatening its independence and security.

The U.S. Government is fully aware of the immense tasks facing the Government of Viet-Nam in its effort to

---

"weak-kneed," and Eisenhower privately lamented that Churchill and Eden showed a "woeful unawareness" of the risks of inaction in Southeast Asia. Dulles misinterpreted Eden's willingness to discuss long-range security arrangements as a tentative commitment to United Action, and when informed of the actual British position, he was incensed. The White House and State Department were outraged by French intransigence. Eisenhower blamed the French for their present plight: they had used "weasel words in promising independence," he wrote a friend, "and through this reason as much as anything else have suffered reverses that have been inexcusable." He refused to consider intervention on France's terms. The French "want us to come in as junior partners and provide materials, etc.,

achieve solidarity, internal security, and economic rehabilitation. The United States has already played an important role in the evacuation of hundreds of thousands of refugees from Communist rule in North Viet-Nam.

Moreover, as the President told Prime Minister Ngo Dinh Diem in his letter of October 23d [1954], U.S. representatives in Viet-Nam have been instructed to consider with the Vietnamese authorities how a program of American aid given directly to Viet-Nam can best assist that country. General Collins will explore this matter with Prime Minister Ngo Dinh Diem and his Government in order to help them resolve their present critical problems and to supplement measures adopted by the Vietnamese themselves.

In executing his temporary mission, General Collins will maintain close liaison with the French Commissioner General, Gen. Paul Ely, for the purpose of exchanging views on how best, under existing circumstances, the freedom and welfare of Viet-Nam can be safeguarded."

Mission of the Special United States Representative in Vietnam: Statement Issued by the White House, November 3, 1954.

while they themselves retain authority in that region," and he would "not go along with them on any such notion."

Congressional opposition reinforced the administration's determination to avoid unilateral intervention. In a speech that won praise from both sides of the aisles, Senator John F. Kennedy, a Democrat from Massachusetts, warned that no amount of military aid could conquer "an enemy of the people which has the support and covert appeal of the people." Victory could not be attained in Indochina as long as France remained. When a "high administration source," subsequently identified as Vice President Richard M. Nixon, remarked "off the record" that if United Action failed, the United States might have to act alone, the reaction was immediate and strong.

Thus, even when France relented a bit, continued British opposition to military intervention settled the fate of United Action. In late April, Foreign Minister Georges Bidault, whom Dulles described as "close to the breaking point," made a last desperate appeal for American support, warning that only a "massive" air attack would save Dienbienphu and hinting that France was prepared to internationalize the war. His hopes of implementing United Action suddenly revived, Dulles informed Bidault that if the British could be persuaded to go along, the administration would seek a congressional resolution authorizing intervention. Over the next three days, the secretary frantically attempted to convert Eden, urgently warning that without support from its allies, France might give up the fight. The British would have none of it, however, and the administration was forced to back off. Eisenhower informed congressional leaders on April 26 that it would be a "tragic error to go in alone as a partner of France" and made it clear that the United States would intervene only as part of a "grouping of interested nations." Three days later, the NSC formally decided to "hold up for the time any military action in Indo China until we see how Geneva is coming along."

It remains difficult to evaluate Eisenhower's handling of the Dienbienphu crisis. Whether he wanted to intervene militarily and was blocked by Congress and the allies or whether United Action was a clever bluff designed to shift blame for nonintervention elsewhere cannot be determined with certainty. If indeed they had made up their minds, Eisenhower and Dulles covered their tracks so skillfully that they confounded contemporaries and baffled future scholars. Thus as [historians] Leslie Gelb and Richard Betts have concluded, they can be charged with "egregious bumbling saved only by the unwillingness of allies to participate and the restraint of enemies," or they can be praised for a "dazzling display of neutralizing potential domestic opposition and of deterring hostile states bent on total victory."

Whatever the case, the decision sealed Dienbienphu's doom. Without U.S. air power, France had no means of saving the fortress. Subjected to merciless pounding from Vietminh artillery and to a series of human-wave assaults, the exhausted and hopelessly outmanned defenders finally surrendered on May 7 after fifty-five days of stubborn but futile resistance. The attention of belligerents and interested outside parties immediately shifted to Geneva, where the following day the Indochina phase of the conference was to begin. Buoyed by its victory, the Vietminh confidently savored the prize for which it had been fighting for more than seven years. Its influence in northern Vietnam reduced to a small pocket around Hanoi, France began preparations to abandon the north and salvage as much as possible in the area below the sixteenth parallel. The French delegation came to Geneva, Bidault lamented, holding a "two of clubs and a three of diamonds."

Steering a Successful Middle Course in Vietnam

Richard H. Immerman

As France's vulnerability in Southeast Asia became more apparent in the spring of 1954 Eisenhower found himself attempting to choose between what he viewed as the "unattainable," total U.S. involvement in a secure Vietnam, and the "unacceptable," the complete withdrawal of U.S. support from the people and government of South Vietnam. Historian Richard H. Immerman argues that Eisenhower was fully aware of the implications of his decision to provide economic and political support to Ngo Dinh Diem's South Vietnamese government. Eisenhower knew that this support would ultimately return to haunt the United States, Immerman maintains, but Eisenhower's decision charted a successful middle course between the extremes of total involvement and total withdrawal. While Eisenhower's decision would have the ultimate effect of leaving the problem of Vietnam for future administrations, that same decision gave the United States breathing room and the time to understand what was happening in Southeast Asia. While not a perfect strategy, Immerman concludes, Eisenhower's partial support of the Diem regime must be understood as successful; later U.S. mistakes in Vietnam were the fault of later, less cautious administrations.

Immerman is a professor of history at Temple University. He is the author and coauthor of many works on U.S. foreign poli-

Excerpted from "Between the Unattainable and the Unacceptable: Eisenhower and Dienbienphu," by Richard H. Immerman, in *Reevaluating Eisenhower: American Foreign Policy in the 1950s*, edited by Richard A. Melanson and David Mayers (Chicago: University of Illinois Press, 1987.) Copyright © 1987 by Richard H. Immerman. Reprinted with permission.

cy, including *John Foster Dulles: Piety, Pragmatism, and Power in United States Foreign Policy* and (with Robert R. Bowie, Eisenhower's assistant secretary of state for policy planning) *Waging Peace: How Eisenhower Shaped an Enduring Cold War Strategy.*

T HE FALL OF THE FRENCH FORTRESS OF DIENBIENPHU TO THE Communist-led Vietminh insurgents on May 7 dismayed many Americans in 1954, and Chairman of the Joint Chiefs of Staff Admiral Arthur Radford was but one of the key Washington actors who regretted that the United States had not provided France with more assistance, even if that assistance included direct military intervention. President Dwight D. Eisenhower himself confided to [British prime minister Edward] Heath that he continued to wonder "whether there was anything he might have done to have persuaded the French to internationalize the Indo-Chinese war." In retrospect, however, after America's subsequent military involvement had resulted in the deaths of close to sixty thousand of its citizens, destroyed the lives of so many more, and nonetheless failed to prevent a Communist victory, the 1954 decision against active intervention took on a much more positive cast. Indeed, with increasing frequency it is cited to illustrate that far from being a bland, do-nothing president, Eisenhower was a shrewd, often devious leader whose perspicacity enabled him to avoid the pitfalls of his successors.

Notwithstanding the prominent role played by the decision not to intervene in this "Eisenhower revisionism," the administration's handling of the Dienbienphu crisis remains shrouded in controversy and confusion. Owing to incomplete or misleading source material, ethnocentric bias, partisanship, or self-interest, scholars, journalists, and memoirists have advanced widely divergent and conflicting interpretations of the complex events. An abundance of recently declassified documents clarifies many of the most salient issues and underscores that none of the previous accounts is wholly sufficient. Because Eisenhower's policy toward Indochina was such a significant episode of his presidency, the new documentation requires its reconsideration.

The situation in Indochina had not reached crisis proportions when Eisenhower took office [in January 1953], and his early national security agenda was crowded with such pressing issues as shaping the New Look defense posture and discussing means to settle the Korean conflict. Still, the administration neither neglected Indochina nor challenged its predecessor's commitment to support the French effort. Less than three weeks into the term Secretary of State John Foster Dulles clearly spelled out the government's position to appropriate representatives from the JCS [Joint Chiefs of Staff] and Mutual Security Administration [MSA]. "If Southeast Asia were lost," Dulles explained, "this would lead to the loss of Japan. The situation of the Japanese is hard enough with China being commie. You would not lose Japan immediately, but from there on out the Japs would be thinking of how to get on the other side."

By March, the JCS had recommended a strategy for keeping the Asian dominoes from failing. Outlining the military's position, Army Chief of Staff General Joseph Collins maintained in a memorandum ominously titled "Broadening the Participation of the United States in the Indochina Operation" that the United States need not become directly involved in the fighting. It would, however, have to provide the French with greater financial and material support. Most important, it must bring pressure on Paris to develop a more effective strategy, to augment the native troops, and to provide the natives with additional incentives by granting them increased autonomy.

Implementing the JCS's recommendations proved extremely difficult. Not only was the budget- and Korean-conscious Congress threatening to cut current appropriations for Indochina, but Paris also resisted appeals to revise its strategy, expand the size and role of the indigenous forces, and agree to the Associated States's independence. "If the French were completely honest they would get out of Indochina," Dulles remarked on the administration's lack of leverage, "and we certainly don't want that." Yet if they continued to balk at the JCS's suggestions, said Air Force Chief General Hoyt Vandenberg in presenting the dilemma's other side, "we will be pouring money down a rathole.". . .

The Middle Course

On April 29 Eisenhower remarked at his press conference that U.S. policy toward Indochina must steer "a course between two extremes, one of which . . . would be unattainable, the other unacceptable." Later that day the NSC [National Security Council] met to decide precisely what that course should be. The discussion began routinely enough, with [CIA Director] Allen Dulles, [Undersecretary of State Walter Beddell] Smith, and Radford briefing the council on recent developments. "A brief interval of silence" followed; the debate erupted. Arguing the case for intervention, MSA administrator Harold Stassen asserted that the United States had no choice but to "go in alone." Congress and the public would support intervention "if the Commander-in-Chief made it clear to them that such a move was necessary to save Southeast Asia from Communism." Eisenhower heard Stassen out, and then accused him of not only misdiagnosing the national temper but also making assumptions that "leaped over situations of grave difficulty." The position of the United States as the leader of the free world necessitated associates. Without allies "the leader is just an adventurer like Genghis Khan." Further, "We would in the eyes of many Asiatic peoples merely replace French colonialism with American colonialism . . . [and] be everywhere accused of imperialistic ambitions." Unilateral intervention, the president continued, "would mean a general war with China and perhaps the USSR, which the United States would have to prosecute separated from its allies." Accordingly, perhaps the NSC should be examining the "great question:" "If our allies were going to fall away in any case it might be better for the United States to leap over the smaller obstacles and hit the biggest one with all the power we had."

Eisenhower had laid it on the line. The United States did have to steer a course between the "unacceptable and the unattainable." Prudence required a trade-off. To [Deputy Secretary of Defense] Roger Kyes, "The President was as sound as anyone could be. The people of the United States would rather hit Soviet Russia than put a single man to fight in Indochina." Stassen, now joined by Nixon and Smith, remained unconvinced. America had to draw the line somewhere. A single air strike might not be decisive at Dienbienphu, they rebutted, but it would signify to the Communists "This is as far as you go, and no further." Once that line had been drawn, France could reassume responsibility. There would be no need for a U.S.-USSR confrontation.

Working with the French

Eisenhower did not disagree. France was the key. If he could be assured that with American and regional support France would reassume responsibility for continuing the war, Eisenhower declared, he would request Congress's authorization. He had not decided against intervention, only against intervention under the present circumstances. Without further controversy, therefore, the Council agreed that "despite the current unwillingness of the British Government to participate at this time and without awaiting developments at the Geneva Conference, the United States should continue . . . to organize a regional grouping, including initially the U.S., France, the Associated States, and other nations with interests in the area, for the defense of Southeast Asia against Communist efforts by any means to gain control of the countries in this area. . . ." Lest any responsible official misunderstand, Cutler elaborated upon the decision at the planning board meeting later that afternoon. "Intervention by U.S. combat forces," he emphasized, "would still depend on invitation of indigenous nations; a sufficient regional grouping so that it would not appear that the U.S. was acting alone to bail out French colonies and to meet Congressional sentiment, and on Congressional authority. *No intervention by executive action*" (added emphasis).

Dienbienphu fell on May 7, the hopelessly outmanned defenders finally surrendering after fifty-five days of heroic resistance. Under the policy guidelines established by Eisenhower and Dulles and confirmed by the NSC, nevertheless, the administration's endeavor to prevent the loss of Indochina, by intervention if necessary, progressed. The State Department drafted another joint congressional resolution authorizing the president to employ air and naval forces in Asia to assist friendly governments "to maintain their authority against subversive and revolutionary efforts fomented by Communist regimes." Discussions were held with the French to plan for military collaboration, the JCS developed a comprehensive concept of operations, and interagency planning continued. Officials even drew up a working paper outlining day-by-day measures that would be taken. In the end, the conditions Eisenhower had deemed essential for intervention to be viable were never met. He never received Paris's necessary assurance that it would maintain responsibility for the war, with or without United Action. Instead, the Laniel government set conditions of its own. If Eisenhower wanted France to continue, he was informed, he would have to make a prior commitment to use ground forces and promise full-fledged intervention if China entered the war. The president conceded a willingness to deploy a limited number of Marines, but he would formally agree only to use air and naval forces. To Washington, Paris's refusing to "internationalize" the war unless the U.S. acceded to its conditions was like "holding a sword of Damocles over our heads."

On June 10, Dulles wrote "As regards internationalization, it should be made clear to the French that our offer does not indefinitely lie on the table to be picked up by them one minute before midnight. . . . I believe we should begin to think of a time limit on our intervention." The limit was one week. On June 16, Dulles told the Senate Foreign Relations Committee that when the administration first proposed United Action, "It then seemed that intervention with some sea and air power, with possibly only a token show of a few marines on land, might be enough to change and alter the situation. . . . Now the situation has become such that successful intervention would be a much more momentous affair from a military standpoint. . . . The French are perfectly well aware that they don't have in any sense any call upon the United States to join the war, even if the war goes on as a result of what happens at Geneva." On June 17, Pierre Mendes-France was elected France's prime minister. Committed to a negotiated settlement, he had no intention of calling upon the United States to join the war. Dulles remarked at that day's NSC that "he thought it best to let the French get out of Indochina entirely and then to try to rebuild from the foundations." Eisenhower agreed and suggested that the council move on to the next item on the agenda.

Before Mendes-France's election, the administration had already prepared itself for a French withdrawal from Indochina and the probable loss of all of Vietnam. Within a week of the fall of Dienbienphu Dulles, in contrast to his previous statements, testified, "We do not want to operate on what has been referred to as the domino theory, where the loss of one area will topple another and another. . . . I think there is a good chance, if we can get some cooperation, to prevent that situation from continuing and that we can, through some collective security or united defense arrangement, which I hope would still include Indochina, prevent the loss of vital areas in Southeast Asia. This is what I am working on at the present time."

Eisenhower Sees Clearly

Hence, while the administration sought United Action in Indochina, it simultaneously sought what would become the Southeast Asia Treaty Organization (SEATO). Ironically, the major unanticipated development was the partition of Vietnam. In a carefully prepared briefing to Congress on May 5, Dulles had maintained that "The most hopeful formula for peace in Vietnam was for an agreement with the Vietminh on the withdrawal of all foreign troops, the establishment of a coalition government, and the holding of elections in six months, all of which would probably result in the loss of Vietnam to the communists. Partition was not a likely solution because either side agreeing to partition of the country would lose the support of the people of the area." The evidence reveals that the administration held to this view and acquiesced to partition only in order to prevent prolonging the Geneva negotiations, a circumstance, it feared, that could lead to further deterioration. Once partition had been effected, however, and Ngo Dinh Diem emerged as a seemingly capable leader, it decided to include South Vietnam, albeit informally, in SEATO. In hindsight this proved to be a gross mistake. Despite his own rationale for not intervening in 1954, Eisenhower did "Americanize" the region and commit U.S. prestige to defend a government which, to use Dulles's phrase, "would lose the support of the people." It had been Eisenhower himself who predicted the consequences. It would be Eisenhower's successors who would have to face them.

Compromising the Domino Theory

Theodore Draper

According to the Eisenhower administration's "domino theory," if Vietnam fell to communism, the rest of Southeast Asia would soon follow. When Communist forces threatened to overwhelm French troops at the Battle of Dien Bien Phu, the Eisenhower administration found itself caught between preventing the spread of communism—as the domino theory indicated it must—and avoiding war in Southeast Asia. In the following selection, Theodore Draper argues that Eisenhower ultimately settled on a poor compromise in which Vietnam was partitioned into a Communist North and a U.S.-supported South. In effect, Eisenhower compromised his domino theory and simply put the problem of what to do about Vietnam off for another day and another administration.

Theodore Draper has been a research fellow at the Hoover Institution on War, Revolution, and Peace at Stanford University and a member of the Institute for Advanced Studies at Princeton. He is the author of numerous works on U.S. history including *The Very Thin Line: The Iran Contra Affairs,* for which he won the 1992 Pulitzer Prize in History.

───────────────────────

THE FRENCH DEFEAT AT DIEN BIEN PHU CONFRONTED THE Eisenhower administration with a difficult and painful decision: Should the United States take the place of France in the Indochinese war?

From "Eisenhower and Vietnam: A Liberal Interpretation," by Theodore Draper, in *The Eisenhower Era: The Age of Consensus,* edited by Paul S. Holbo and Robert W. Sellen (Hinsdale, IL: The Dryden Press, 1974). Copyright © 1974 by The Dryden Press. Reprinted with permission.

Abstractly, Eisenhower and Dulles did not give themselves much choice. They were the first to apply the "domino theory" to Southeast Asia and even beyond. On April 7, 1954, President Eisenhower gave official status to what he then called the "'falling domino' principle." It implied that the loss of Indochina would inevitably cause the fall of the rest of Southeast Asia like a "row of dominoes." Secretary Dulles tried to convince British Foreign Secretary Anthony Eden that the loss of Indochina would lead to the eventual loss of Thailand, Malaya, Burma, and Indonesia. This prospect seemed so alarming that leading figures in the Eisenhower administration advocated American military intervention in Vietnam to prevent it.

The outstanding "hawks" in 1953 and 1954 were Vice President Nixon, Secretary of State Dulles, and [Chair of the Joint Chiefs of Staff] Admiral Radford. Nixon told the American Society of Newspaper Editors on April 16, 1954, that it was necessary to "take the risk now by putting our boys in" to avoid further Communist expansion in Asia and Indochina. Dulles also spoke publicly in favor of taking "serious risks." In March, Dulles told Eden, the United States Chiefs of Staff had suggested intervening in Vietnam with American naval and air forces. Even the possible use of atomic weapons, it is said, was raised in some fashion. According to General Matthew B. Ridgway, then the Army's Chief of Staff, "we very nearly found ourselves involved in a bloody jungle war in which our nuclear capability would have been almost useless." General Ridgway also recorded that "individuals of great influence, both in and out of government," raised the cry for United States intervention "to come to the aid of France with arms."

Opposition to Intervention

But the hawkish wing of the Administration met with determined opposition from at least three directions. Despite—or perhaps because of—his military background, President

Eisenhower was most sensitive to Congressional approval of so serious a step as getting into an Asian war. In Congress the Nixon-Dulles-Radford line of military intervention encountered an extremely cold reception. Two of the most powerful and most conservative Senators came out strongly against an interventionist policy. One of them was Democratic Senator Richard B. Russell of Georgia, chairman of the key Armed Services Committee, a Southern patrician who was able to make or break both legislation and careers in the upper house. Later, Senator Russell recalled that he had been visited by Assistant Secretary of State Thurston B. Morton, who informed him of President Eisenhower's decision to assist the South Vietnamese. Senator Russell told Morton that he "feared this course would be costly in blood and treasure," though, once it was decided on, he "had no alternative but to support the flag." Another conservative Southern Senator who strongly opposed the Eisenhower decision on the Senate floor in 1954 was Democratic Senator John Stennis of Mississippi. According to Stennis, the first two hundred American Air Force mechanics, sent to South Vietnam early in 1954, were temporarily withdrawn as a result of Congressional objections. In his memoirs Eisenhower recalls that these two Senators were "uneasy about any American participation whatever," and he informed Secretary of State Dulles: "They fear that this may be opening the door to increased and unwise introduction of American troops into that area."

At a secret meeting on April 3, 1954, five senior Senators and three Representatives made known their apprehensions to Secretary Dulles and Admiral Radford. One of those who asked the most searching and embarrassing questions was the then Democratic Minority Leader, Senator Lyndon B. Johnson. He appeared to take the position that the United States could not intervene in Vietnam without allies and forced the Secretary of State to admit that he had not as yet even consulted them. Thus Lyndon

Johnson's first important contribution to American policy in Vietnam tended to encourage restraint. Yet, with the fall of Dien Bien Phu the following month, Senator Johnson spoke publicly in quite another vein. He made the French defeat into the most "stunning reversal" ever suffered by American foreign policy "in all its history." He mourned that "we have been caught bluffing by our enemies" and had made our friends and Allies "frightened and wondering, as we do, where we are heading." The United States, he said, stood "in clear danger of being left naked and alone in a hostile world." Then, unaccountably, instead of advising his listeners to meet the danger in the world, he said that the prospect was so terribly painful "that we should turn our eyes from abroad and look homeward." It was, of course, a strictly partisan, rhetorical performance at a fund-raising dinner for his party in Washington, and only the fact that it was made by the future President in another Vietnamese crisis has invested it with any significance. Still, if this is what Senator Johnson thought of the responsibility that President Eisenhower bore for a *French* defeat, one wonders what Senator Johnson would have said of all the *American* setbacks and frustrations suffered by President Johnson.

After the April 3 meeting with the congressional leaders, however, Mr. Dulles did not give up so easily. He hit on the idea that he could sell his plan to Congress if he could make American intervention part of a larger "collective effort." For this purpose he needed the agreement and cooperation of Great Britain. On April 11, 1954, almost a month before the fall of Dien Bien Phu, Dulles went to London to convince Prime Minister Churchill and Foreign Secretary Eden. He tried out all the arguments which have become so familiar—the "domino theory" and historical analogies from the 1930s. The situation in Indochina, Dulles told Eden, "was analogous to the Japanese invasion of Manchuria in 1931 and to Hitler's reoccupation of the

Rhineland." But Churchill and Eden refused to be persuaded. Churchill even saw through Dulles' game and confided to Eden that what the British "were being asked to do was to assist in misleading Congress into approving a military operation, which would in itself be ineffective, and might well bring the world to the verge of a major war."

Finally, opposition came from an unexpected quarter—the United States Army's high command, General Ridgway and General James M. Gavin, Chief of Plans and Development, took the position that the United States could hold on to Indochina, but that it was not worth the price that would have to be paid. An Army team of experts in every field was sent to Indochina to study the ramifications of a major intervention. The Army leaders, General Gavin related, projected the need for eight infantry divisions, plus about thirty-five engineer battalions. General Ridgway told Republican Senator George D. Aiken of Vermont that even if 2 million men were sent to Vietnam, they would "be swallowed up."

Thus the interventionist pressure from Vice President Nixon, Secretary of State Dulles, Admiral Radford, and others was more than offset by the reluctance of influential Senators, the disapproval of the British, and the misgivings of the Army command. This formidable opposition was too much for the innately prudent Eisenhower, whose most popular move was to get us out of one Asian war and who was now confronted with the demand to get us into another one. The line-up of forces was not lost on his Secretary of State.

Dulles's Maneuvering

Dulles was an extraordinarily artful diplomatist. He habitually reversed Theodore Roosevelt's advice about speaking softly and carrying a big stick. The Dulles method consisted of using strong words to hide inner weaknesses. He was a progenitor of the "domino theory," according to which a

French defeat in Indochina would be fatal in the whole of Southeast Asia and beyond. Yet, when attempts were made to pin him down, he refused to subscribe to the full implications of his own theory. In order to make the "domino theory" inoperative, he expounded, it was only necessary to form a "collective-security arrangement" in Southeast Asia. Moreover, he added, "I do not want to give the impression either that if events that we could not control and which we do not anticipate should lead to their [the states of Indochina] being lost, that we would consider the whole situation hopeless, and we would give up in despair." On another occasion, on May 11, 1954, Dulles was specifically asked whether he thought the Southeast Asia area could be held without Indochina. He answered: "I do." This was not exactly orthodox "domino theory," but it served to give Dulles a safe line of retreat. Dulles succeeded in patching together a Southeast Asia Treaty Organization (SEATO)—composed of France, Britain, Australia, New Zealand, Thailand, the Philippines, Pakistan, and the United States—in September 1954, too late to prevent the French domino from falling in Indochina.

Once United States military intervention was doomed, Dulles hedged it about with so many conditions that he was in no danger of ever seeing it brought about. He propounded no fewer than five conditions as the necessary justification for intervention: (1) an invitation from the French; (2) clear assurance of complete independence to Laos, Cambodia, and Vietnam; (3) evidence of concern by the United Nations; (4) a collective effort on the part of other nations in the area; and (5) assurance that France would not itself withdraw from the battle until it was won. None of these conditions were, in the circumstances of 1954, likely to be completely satisfied, and Dulles would probably have added a few others if he had thought that these might be accepted.

The last American stand at the Geneva Conference was

exquisitely Dullesian. First, Dulles professed to regard with holy horror any agreement which handed over more people and territory to a Communist regime. As a result, the United States refused to sign the Geneva Agreements. But then Under Secretary of State Bedell Smith was authorized to declare that the United States would "refrain from any threat or use of force to disturb" the agreements and "would view any renewal of the aggression in violation of the aforesaid agreements with grave concern and as seriously threatening international peace and security." After it was all over, though over eighteen million people of North Vietnam had been "handed over" to the Communists, President Eisenhower opined that the Geneva settlement had not been so bad after all; it was, he wrote in his memoirs, "the best" the French "could get under the circumstances" and he even "saw the beginning of development of better understanding between the Western powers and the nations of Southeast Asia." And Secretary Dulles later confided his thoughts about the agreements to a favorite American magazine; one of these was that handing over half of Vietnam to the Communists had actually "eliminated the possibility of a domino effect in Southeast Asia" by "saving" the other half, Laos and Cambodia. . . .

The proponents of the 1954 "domino theory" were not prepared to think through and live up to their own doctrine. If, as President Eisenhower asserted, the French loss of Indochina would cause the fall of Southeast Asia "like a set of dominoes," and, as others did not fail to add, the fall of Southeast Asia would cause the loss of huge areas as far away as India, the stakes were so high that the advocates of this theory were obliged to take the most "serious risks," without the impossible conditions posed by Secretary Dulles. Not only did Eisenhower back away from the implications of his own theory but also the immediate consequences of the French defeat did not bear out his dire foreboding.

McCARTHYISM
AND
PRESIDENTIAL
SILENCE

Eisenhower's Decision to Remain Silent: A Successful Tactic

Robert J. Donovan

When Eisenhower took office in 1952 he knew that Senator Joseph McCarthy of Wisconsin was going to pose a problem for his administration. McCarthy was a member of Eisenhower's political party, but he and Eisenhower had radically different political beliefs. When McCarthy began a crusade against communism in the United States—and began attacking Eisenhower himself—members of Eisenhower's staff urged the president to confront the senator openly. Although he disapproved of and detested McCarthy, however, Eisenhower decided that the president ought to remain above such partisan squabbles. "I am not," he declared, "going to get down in the gutter with that guy." In this excerpt from *Eisenhower: The Inside Story*, Robert J. Donovan argues that while Eisenhower's silence was disturbing, the president was justified in not openly confronting McCarthy.

During the Eisenhower administration Robert J. Donovan was the White House correspondent for the *New York Herald Tribune*. He is the author of many books on U.S. politicians, including the best seller *PT 109: John F. Kennedy in World War II* and *Tumultuous Years: The Presidency of Harry S. Truman*.

MCCARTHY OPENED THE FIRST OF HIS MAJOR OFFENSIVES against the Eisenhower administration in a national radio and television broadcast on November 24, 1953. The networks had given him free time to answer Truman's use of the word "McCarthyism" in the former President's speech eight days earlier defending his conduct in the Harry Dexter White case. McCarthy first fired some salvos back at Independence, Missouri, and then swung his guns around toward the White House and the State Department. While the Eisenhower administration was doing "infinitely" better than Truman and Acheson, he said, there were "a few cases where our batting average is zero—we struck out."

He singled out two examples. One was that John Paton Davies, Jr., a controversial career diplomat, who had been cleared seven times by State Department loyalty boards and once by the old Loyalty Review Board, was still in the department as counselor at the United States Embassy in Lima, Peru. The other was that the Eisenhower administration had failed to liquidate the "foulest bankruptcy" of the Truman administration. McCarthy listed this as the continuance of mutual assistance to Britain while the British traded with Red China, the jailer of American flyers and soldiers captured during the Korean War.

> Are we going to continue to send perfumed notes? [McCarthy demanded] . . . it is time that we, the Republican Party, liquidate this blood-stained blunder . . . we promised the American people something different. Let us deliver—not next year or next month—let us deliver now. . . . We can do this by merely saying to our allies and alleged allies, "If you continue to ship to Red China . . . you will not get one cent of American money."

McCarthy also took direct issue with Eisenhower, who at his press conference the preceding week, as it happened, had protested that he did not know what the term Mc-

Carthyism meant. At that same press conference the President had said he was confident that the administration's routing of subversives would prove so thorough that the Communists-in-government issue would have no place in the 1954 campaign.

McCarthy gruffly disagreed. The "raw, harsh, unpleasant fact" was, he told his national audience, that "Communism is an issue and will be an issue in 1954."

In public Eisenhower continued to hold himself aloof from McCarthy. In private he could go up in an utter blaze over him. McCarthy's tactics disgusted and infuriated him. On the one hand, he was frustrated by McCarthy's impregnability—a President cannot remove a Senator. On the other, he was torn by conflicting advice. His friend and former political lieutenant, Paul G. Hoffman, chairman of the board of the Studebaker-Packard Corporation, for instance, was urging him to let McCarthy have it with both barrels. Contrary advice came from the Vice-President [Richard Nixon], who warned Eisenhower that a personal frontal attack on McCarthy might lead the President into the vicious situation that had embroiled Truman and Acheson. The White House staff itself had been split right down the middle on the question, and McCarthy's speech revived and rather bitterly intensified the difference.

Disagreement over How to Handle McCarthy

On November 27 [Special Assistant to the President C.D.] Jackson sent a memorandum to [former New Hampshire Governor Sherman] Adams saying that watching the McCarthy telecast had been an "exceptionally horrible experience." Here, he said, was an open declaration of war by a Republican Senator upon a Republican President. This opinion expressed privately by Jackson was widely held in public. *The Commonweal*, for example, commented that the speech "actually contained Senator McCarthy's public declaration of war upon the present administration." Jackson wanted the President to repudiate McCarthy as a Republican. He wanted him to do so at his very next press conference, which was to be held on December 2.

On the same side as Jackson in this dispute, actively or passively, were such members of the staff as [Press Secretary James C.] Hagerty, [Administrative Assistant] Bryce N. Harlow, Charles F. Willis, Jr., Tom Stephens, [Special Assistant to the President for National Security Affairs Robert] Cutler and Stanley M. Rumbough, Jr. A man of strong opinions with a strong personality behind them, Jackson had argued that the President was morally involved in the McCarthy issue and no longer could stand aside. He maintained that McCarthy was an irresponsible politician with whom it was impossible to come to terms in any case. "Appeasing" McCarthy, he argued, was useless. Sooner or later McCarthy was going to war on the administration, he said, and when that day came, it would be better for the administration to have been on the offensive than suddenly to have to dig a defensive position.

On the opposite side were members of the staff who, by and large had had a great deal of previous experience on Capitol Hill and whose jobs in the White House involved the handling of relations with Congress. This group included [Deputy Assistant to the President] General Persons, [Appointment Secretary Bernard M.] Shanley, Gerald D. Morgan, I. Jack Martin, Earle D. Chesney, [Former Massachusetts Senator Henry Cabat] Lodge and Homer H. Gruenther, brother of General Gruenther, and siding with them usually was Adams.

Their contention was that it would only make matters worse for the President in Congress if he engaged in a personal quarrel with McCarthy. They could foresee no end to such a row. Neither could they see how the President could out-brawl McCarthy. Once a personal Eisenhower-McCarthy fight began, they feared, it would sunder the Republican ranks and thereby jeopardize the President's leadership and his program. . . .

Without mentioning McCarthy by name, Dulles said that the Senator's criticism "attacks the very heart of U.S. foreign policy." It was the "clear and firm purpose" of the administration, the Secretary said, to treat other free nations as sovereign equals, helping them but not assuming that this help gave the United States the right to dictate their trade policies or "make them our satellites." To deter the Soviets from atomic attack, he continued, the United States must always be ready "to retaliate with a devastating blow against the vitals of Russia." The potentiality for such retaliation existed, he said, "only because we share the well-located bases of other friendly countries."

Before Eisenhower's press conference the next morning, his staff met with the President to draw up a statement he intended to read to the reporters. Jackson came with a proposed Presidential statement he had drafted, attacking McCarthy by name. The President put on his spectacles, took a look at it and banged it down on the desk.

"I will not get in the gutter with that guy," he told Jackson angrily.

Many times in those days Eisenhower made this same point: To fight McCarthy, either he would have to descend to McCarthy's level or else bring McCarthy up to the President's level, and he would not do either one. . . .

The Army-McCarthy Hearings Proved Critical

[A] new rumpus began after the Army gave each member of McCarthy's subcommittee on March 11 a copy of a report charging that McCarthy and Roy Cohn, chief counsel to the group, had made many threats to Army officials to get a commission and other favored treatment for Private David Schine. Schine, who had been Cohn's sidekick on the seriocomic junket across Europe investigating the overseas information service a year before, was a subcommittee consultant, who had been drafted into the Army in November, 1953.

The report, which the Army had prepared at the suggestion of Sherman Adams, was in the form of a chronology of alleged threats and intrusions by McCarthy and Cohn on behalf of Schine. It alleged, for example, that upon learning that Schine might be sent overseas, Cohn had warned that this would "wreck the Army" and undo [Robert T.] Stevens as Secretary [of the Army]; that Cohn had threatened to "expose the Army in its worst light"; that Cohn had tried to get Schine relieved from Sunday KP, and that McCarthy had asked Stevens to give Schine the military assignment of studying the "pro-Communist leanings in West Point textbooks."

McCarthy countercharged that the report was "blackmail" to force the subcommittee to end its investigation of the Army. He said that Stevens had tried to shake the subcommittee off the Army's trail by urging the investigators to go after the Navy and the Air Force instead, a statement Stevens hotly denied.

In the Cabinet on March 12, Nixon reviewed the background of the Army's charges. If the report was correct, he said, his own personal conviction was that the Republicans should take the initiative in dismissing Cohn as counsel.

On April 2 the Cabinet was discussing the wire-tapping bill and other measures on the President's program to combat subversion.

"Bad thing about McCarthy," Eisenhower said, "is that he is impeding this work."

In view of this, the President added, but more in jest than seriously, it might be a good idea for the Kremlin to put McCarthy on its payroll.

The White House did what it could to throw the investigation from McCarthy's subcommittee into the Senate Armed Services Committee where McCarthy's influence would have been much less strong. The efforts failed, however, partly because Saltonstall, who was chairman of Armed Services, wanted nothing to do with this hot potato. He was facing a fight for re-election in Massachusetts the following November, and he could see nothing but trouble with the Irish Catholic vote if he got entangled with McCarthy. The Permanent Investigations Subcommittee retained jurisdiction, but with McCarthy temporarily relinquishing the chairmanship to his friend, Senator Karl E. Mundt, Republican, of South Dakota.

The televised hearings began on April 22 with an ineffable cast of characters that included McCarthy and Stevens, Cohn and Schine, Francis P. Carr, the pudgy director of the subcommittee staff; John G. Adams, the gaunt counselor of the Army; Ray H. Jenkins, long-jawed Tennessee trial lawyer, who was counsel to the subcommittee; and Joseph N. Welch, a witty and polished Boston attorney, who was counsel to the Army.

For thirty-six days the hearings were the national business, the national pastime and, as some said, the national disgrace. For Eisenhower these five weeks were a period of acute embarrassment, anger, impatience and frustration. Until he came to the White House he had lived a lifetime in the Army. Pride, loyalty and devotion to the Army are second nature with him. The Army has a strong emotional hold on him. One small insight into his sentiment shows up in the fact that while in office he has never attended an Army-Navy football game, as his predecessors did, because he has felt physically incapable of displaying the impartiality between the teams that is expected of the Commander-in-Chief.

A lot of Army men were hurt inside their hearts, he had remarked during the Peress case. The same could be said of his own feelings during the televised hearings. That in his administration Army officers and Army affairs should have been dragged before the public eye in the tumultuous, disorderly and acrimonious manner of these proceedings galled him. His resentment over the airing of haggles involving the Secretary of the Army and a private was boundless. A President seldom speaks with more revealing contempt in public than Eisenhower did at his press conference on April 29 when he referred to Schine as "this private."

When a reporter asked him that day how, as a former commanding general of the Army, he felt about the privileges that had been accorded to Schine, he was almost overpowered by emotion. He asked to be excused from answering. The whole business, he pleaded, was nothing to talk about.

"I just hope it is all concluded very quickly—that's all," he said, starting out of the room even before the conference had been formally ended.

"Our only hope now," the President said at his next press conference, "is that America may derive from this incident advantages that are at least comparable to what we have suffered in loss of international prestige, and, I venture to say, judging from my correspondence, national respect—self-respect. Now that is just about the way I look at it. . . ."

McCarthy Was Condemned and Censured

So far no one has ever discovered any such advantages, but one very important result, indirect yet bound up inextricably with the Army-McCarthy hearings, was that the following December the Senate voted to condemn McCarthy for conduct unbecoming a Senator. This grave action, rare in American history, all but obliterated McCarthy's power to offer further serious challenge to President Eisenhower under foreseeable circumstances.

Two days after the vote was cast the President offered his warm congratulations to Senator Arthur V. Watkins, Republican, of Utah, chairman of the special Senate committee which heard the charges against McCarthy and recommended censure. The President told Watkins at a White

House meeting that he had done a "splendid" job. Three days later McCarthy apologized to the American people for having advocated Eisenhower's election.

Eisenhower's Approach to McCarthy Was Not Well Planned

An assumption that many observers have made is that Eisenhower pursued a conscious strategy of giving McCarthy enough rope to let him hang himself. If true, McCarthy's downfall in December, 1954, proved the President's course a very shrewd and canny one.

Very shrewd it may have been. The fact is, however, that most, although not all, of those who were closest to this problem in the White House do not believe that the President followed any carefully planned, deliberate strategy toward McCarthy. In their opinion it was an attitude rather than a strategy that guided him. If there is any single word that can epitomize this attitude, it is disdain.

The President felt that McCarthy's motives were neither sincere nor inspired by the national interest. He considered his tirades and his reckless charges against individuals despicable in a United States Senator.

During the most exasperating moments that McCarthy inflicted upon him, Eisenhower never believed that McCarthy represented a lasting sentiment of the American people. Even in January, 1954, when a Gallup poll showed that public approval of McCarthy had climbed sixteen points in six months, the President was convinced that this popularity had been fanned by emotionalism and would give way in the end to American common sense. He did not share the concern of many persons that McCarthy could usurp executive powers.

In the face of this high emotion, he believed, the President should act to calm public opinion and not to excite it further by rowing with McCarthy. The national state of mind being what it was at the time, he also saw the further danger that an Eisenhower attack on McCarthy might play straight into McCarthy's hands, putting McCarthy in the role of an underdog being kicked by the President while he was in the very act of saving America from Communism.

The public, of course, could not be privy to Eisenhower's thoughts at that time, and while the Senator was riding high, the President's aloofness left a discouraging void in the movement against McCarthy. To the people—and there were many—who believed that the most important problem in America then was to flatten McCarthy, the President's attitude was so unsatisfying as to be almost unendurable. Yet in view of the fate that overtook the Senator from Wisconsin, a very strong case can be made for it.

Eisenhower's Appropriate Tolerance of McCarthy

Merlo J. Pusey

Eisenhower proved to be a popular and skilled campaigner during the summer of 1952, while he was running for his first term as president. Intent on running an effective and unified government, Eisenhower routinely appeared alongside Republican candidates seeking local and state offices whenever he spoke on the campaign trail. When he arrived in Wisconsin, however, he was faced with the difficult question of whether or not to support Senator Joseph McCarthy for reelection. In this excerpt from *Eisenhower the President*, Merlo J. Pusey argues that Eisenhower made the correct decision in extending cautious support for McCarthy's Republican affiliation while refusing to praise McCarthy's furtherance of the "Red Scare." As a national party leader, Pusey maintains, Eisenhower had no authority to interfere in any way with the senatorial campaign in Wisconsin apart from declaring his support for a mostly Republican slate of candidates. In the end, he suggests, Eisenhower's tactics prevented his presidency from degenerating into factional disputes. Pusey is the author of several books on U.S. history, including *The USA Astride the Globe* and a Pulitzer Prize–winning biography of Supreme Court Chief Justice Charles Evans Hughes.

Excerpted from *Eisenhower the President*, by Merlo J. Pusey (New York: Macmillan, 1956). Copyright © 1956 by Merlo J. Pusey. Renewed by Merlo J. Pusey, 1984. Reprinted with permission.

S ENATOR JOSEPH R. MCCARTHY'S RECORD AS AN UN-
scrupulous investigator and a purveyor of reckless
charges made him obnoxious to . . . General [Eisenhower]
long before they had met. McCarthyism was the antithesis
of what Eisenhower stood for. But the new party leader was
in no position to interfere with the selection of a senatorial candidate in Wisconsin. President [Franklin D.] Roosevelt's attempt to purge several Democratic candidates
seeking Senate and House seats in 1938 had been notori-
ously unsuccessful, and in any event Ike felt that the Republican voters of Wisconsin should select their own senatorial candidate. All he could do was to make clear that he
had no sympathy with the tactics McCarthy used.

Ike's attitude was disclosed through a number of press
conferences in Denver. His position in regard to three controversial items defined the gulf between him and the Mc-
Carthy faction. First, he asserted that the United States' intervention in Korea had been a necessary response to
aggression, while the extremists denounced it as "Truman's
war." Second, he publicly defended [former Secretary of
State] General Marshall against vicious right-wing attacks
on his patriotism. Third, he insisted that, in ousting subversives from government, only fair methods be used. He
refused to give "blanket support" to anyone whose views
would "violate my conception of what is decent, right, just
and fair." In his American Legion speech he assailed the
"assassins of character and the promoters of witch hunts"
as being "dangerous to our freedom at home and to our
world position of leadership."

McCarthy at Arm's Length

When Eisenhower campaigned through Indiana in Sep-
tember [1952], he kept his endorsement of Senator
William Jenner lukewarm by not mentioning his name.
But he was keenly aware of the fact that Jenner had won the
Republican senatorial nomination and was campaigning

for the national ticket. Ike felt that this entitled the senator to nominal support. It seemed probable, moreover, that with a Republican Administration in power, the superpatriots would curb their recklessness if not their zeal in Red-baiting. Eisenhower felt that, without embracing them, he had to give them a chance to accept his leadership in making a new approach to the subversion problem.

McCarthy was similarly kept at arm's length. Eisenhower refused to comment on the senator's sweeping victory in the Wisconsin Republican primary. In early October, however, when the Eisenhower "Look-Ahead-Neighbor" special headed for Milwaukee, the McCarthy issue had to be faced in a more direct fashion.

[Wisconsin] Governor Walter J. Kohler, Jr., and McCarthy boarded the train at Peoria, Illinois. Photographers tried without success to get Ike to pose with McCarthy in the rear car. At the first stop, in Green Bay on the morning of October 3rd, McCarthy was introduced to a cheering crowd before Eisenhower appeared. When the General spoke, he explained his call for the election of the entire Republican ticket by saying that he would need a united team in Washington.

"The differences between me and Senator McCarthy are well known to him and to me, and we have discussed them," he said.

"I want to make one thing very clear. The purposes that he and I have of ridding this Government of the incompetents, the dishonest, and above all the subversives and the disloyal are one and the same. Our differences, therefore, have nothing to do with the end result that we are seeking. The differences apply to method. . . ."

Ike went on to say that the responsibility for ousting subversives from the Government rested squarely on the executive department, and pledged himself to vigilance in carrying out the task.

As the train sped on, Governor Adams asked Governor

Kohler to look over the speech that Eisenhower would deliver that night in Milwaukee. Kohler and his executive secretary, Phillip T. Drotning, suggested a number of minor changes to give the speech more of a Wisconsin flavor. Then Kohler voiced his concern over an isolated paragraph which made a spirited defense of General Marshall against a charge of treason. It was obviously aimed at McCarthy without naming him. Kohler said the paragraph should be taken out because it added nothing to Ike's demand for intelligence and discretion in handling the Communist issue, because it might unnecessarily emphasize a split in the party, and because he felt that the General was attempting to defend his old friend against a charge which had never been made.

The Wisconsin governor produced a clipping from the *Freeman* quoting McCarthy in the *Congressional Record* to the effect that he did not question General Marshall's loyalty but the loyalty of those who gave him orders for his mission to China. This was an unwarranted dilution of McCarthy's charge that Marshall had "made common cause with Stalin" at Teheran [in 1943] and had led a "conspiracy" to let the United States "fall victim to Soviet intrigue."

If McCarthy's speech, which had been made in the Senate on June 14, 1951, did not allege treason, it specified imaginary crimes that were indistinguishable from it. But the question at hand was not whether McCarthy had indulged in offensive conduct; it was whether the party standard-bearer should undertake to discipline a senatorial candidate running on the same ticket in his own state. Ike's advisers agreed that he should not.

As soon as revision of the speech was completed, General Eisenhower, Adams, Kohler, and General Persons held a final consultation in Adams's drawing room. Adams began quoting McCarthy's apologia from the *Freeman* clipping. Ike broke in to ask:

"Are you trying to suggest that I take out that paragraph on Marshall?"

"That's right, General," Adams replied.

"Well, take it out!" the General said in a cooperative mood. "I covered that subject thoroughly in Colorado Springs a few weeks ago."

Eisenhower's Response Was Appropriate

At no time was McCarthy present at this meeting, and he did not see a copy of the speech until after it had been delivered. The decision to take out the reference to General Marshall was made by Eisenhower himself without any urging from anyone. Though he was doubtless influenced by a desire to avoid open offense to McCarthy in his home state, he yielded nothing in principle because his faith in General Marshall had already been clearly stated and would be reiterated later in the campaign.

Moreover, as the speech was delivered in Milwaukee, it made no concession to the McCarthy method of fighting Communism. It was a hard-hitting denunciation of those who had permitted Communist infiltration into the Government and of Adlai Stevenson for joking about this menace to security. "We have had enough," Eisenhower said, "of men who seem to feel that freedom can do nothing but fret and whine as it watches its own slow sure death." Although he was severe in his assault upon the Truman Administration, he held fast to the principle that freedom must defend itself with care and fairness to avoid self-destruction. "We would have nothing left to defend," he declared, "if we allowed ourselves to be swept into any spirit of violent vigilantism."

Before and after the Milwaukee speech many devoted followers urged Ike to throw his scorn for indiscriminate slander into McCarthy's teeth, and some of them parted company with him when he failed to do so. But this did not divert him from his chosen middle course. To the end he persisted in refusing to assail candidates of his own party and in promising that his own methods of fighting Communism would be "the methods of decency, of fairness, and of law."

After the heat of the campaign passed, the wisdom of his course was widely acknowledged. Under our two-party system, party leaders must have a broad tolerance for non-conformists, demagogues, and fanatics. Ike genuinely feared that an attempt on his part to enforce uniformity or to discipline the extremists within his party would lead to the sort of splintering that bedevils most European countries. Beyond this, he was loath to see the program for which he stood founder on the rocks of factionalism. His success in previous great undertakings had come from binding diverse groups together. By clinging to this technique, which is deeply rooted in the nature of the man, he demonstrated a peculiar fitness for leadership in an era of fanaticism and hysteria. Our abhorrence of Communism should unite us, he insisted, and not waste our energies through futile bickering.

A Major Blot on the Presidency

James T. Patterson

After assuming the presidency, Eisenhower was immediately faced with the question of what to do about Senator Joseph McCarthy and his allegations that Communists were attempting to seize control of the U.S. government. While Eisenhower firmly believed that McCarthy was acting solely to gain power, he resolved not to interfere in congressional politics, and so failed to speak out against McCarthy's actions. In this excerpt from *Grand Expectations: The United States, 1945–1974*, historian James T. Patterson argues that Eisenhower's failure to challenge McCarthy's behavior directly was a "major moral blot" on the Eisenhower presidency. While McCarthy's ultimate destruction may have confirmed the efficacy of Eisenhower's strategy, Patterson maintains that Eisenhower should have spent some of his political capital and personal popularity in order to counter McCarthy's accusations. Patterson is a professor of history at Brown University and the author of *America's Struggle Against Poverty in the Twentieth Century* and *Brown v. Board of Education: A Civil Rights Milestone and Its Troubled Legacy*.

THE ULTIMATE TEST OF EISENHOWER'S APPROACH TO LOY-alty and security was of course the question of McCarthy. Once the GOP regained control of the Senate, McCarthy was in his element, for he now had a chair-

Excerpted from *Grand Expectations: The United States, 1945–1974*, by James T. Patterson (New York: Oxford University Press, 1996). Copyright © 1996 by Oxford University Press, Inc. Reprinted with permission.

manship—of the Permanent Subcommittee on Investigations—from which he launched probes that irritated the new administration. Assisting him was a subcommittee staff headed by chief counsel Roy Cohn, a sour, troubled, and fervently anti-Communist attorney. In April 1953 Cohn and a close friend, G. David Schine, set off on a well-publicized tour of Europe in which they called for the purging of allegedly subversive literature from government libraries. The State Department panicked and issued a directive excluding books and works of art by "Communists, fellow travelers, et cetera" from United States information centers abroad. A few books were actually burned.

Eisenhower had never cared for McCarthy, and he fumed when the senator considered contesting the confirmation of Walter Bedell Smith, a close friend who had been Ike's chief of staff in the army, as Undersecretary of State early in 1953. By then Ike was becoming increasingly friendly with Taft, GOP leader in the Senate, and Taft managed to get Smith confirmed. Meanwhile, the President tried quietly to undermine McCarthy in other ways: encouraging GOP senators to oppose him; getting a reluctant Vice-President Nixon to stave off McCarthy's probes into network television; trying to prevent McCarthy from speaking at party gatherings; and suggesting (very indirectly) to publishers and other media executives that they give the rampant senator less time and space. Fred Greenstein, a political scientist, later cited these moves as evidence for what he called Eisenhower's shrewd, subtle, and effective "hidden-hand presidency."

Eisenhower Holds Back

Eisenhower, however, refused to go beyond indirection or to challenge McCarthy head-on. There were several reasons for his reluctance to do battle. First, he agreed with many of McCarthy's goals. As his policies made clear, he was a staunch Cold Warrior. Second, he feared an intraparty brawl that would further imperil his shaky GOP majorities in Congress. McCarthy, after all, was a Republican, and the President was leader of the party. Third, Eisenhower recognized that a direct confrontation with McCarthy would give the rambunctious, often uncontrollable senator even more publicity—on which McCarthy thrived—than he already had. It was better, he thought, to try to ignore him and to hope that given enough rope the senator would eventually hang himself. Eisenhower, finally, was afraid that a fight with McCarthy would diminish the all-important dignity of the presidency. Why use up vital presidential resources to scrap with an alley-fighter? "I will not get into the gutter with that guy," he said privately. Later in the year he added—again privately—"I just won't get into a pissing contest with that skunk."

Ike's worries about the dignity of the presidential office rested on two even deeper concerns. One was to protect his own personal popularity with the American people. Eisenhower, while self-confident, nonetheless craved popular approval. He generally avoided tough decisions that might threaten it. Second, Ike very much wanted to promote domestic tranquility. Throughout his presidency he feared to take actions that might undermine what he considered to be the harmony of American society. He also believed that his mission should be to restrain the role of government, not to force it to fulfill great goals or obligations. These aspirations—protecting his own standing, sustaining domestic tranquility, and curbing the activity of the State—complemented one another in his mind and helped to explain why he often chose *not* to do potentially controversial things: advance ambitious social programs, push for civil rights, get involved in war in Vietnam. They also accounted for his restrained approach to McCarthy. To wade into the arena with such a demagogue, he thought, would endanger his popularity, incite discord, and damage social harmony.

Eisenhower Could Have Done More

Whether Eisenhower should have been more bold remains one of the most contested questions about his presidency. As it turned out, McCarthy did overreach himself and crash in mid-1954. The President thereby stayed out of the gutter. And his personal popularity—always high—did not suffer. On the other hand, these were in many ways dispiriting times. Federal employees, whom Eisenhower was supposed to protect, were hurt under his watch. If Ike had risked even a little of his immense personal popularity and presidential prestige, he might have slowed the senator down or hastened his demise. It could not have hurt him much to try. His refusal to challenge McCarthy represented a major moral blot on his presidency.

No One Spoke Out

Marquis Childs

In this excerpt from his best-selling *Eisenhower: Captive Hero*, Marquis Childs argues that Eisenhower had a naive view of the role of the president in the American political process, which led him to error in failing to challenge Senator Joseph McCarthy directly. The author maintains that Eisenhower's failure to counter McCarthy's wild accusations caused near-irreparable damage to American scientific and social experimentation and development. Childs was the former chief Washington correspondent for the *St. Louis Post-Dispatch* and received the first-ever awarded Pulitzer Prize for Distinguished Commentary in 1969. Childs is the author of the best-selling *The Peacemakers* and *Sweden: The Middle Way.*

———————

AFTER EMBRACING MCCARTHY AND [INDIANA SENATOR William E.] Jenner in the [1952 presidential] campaign, the President may have expected them to be loyal players on the Eisenhower team. But almost at once it became evident that he was doomed to disappointment, as the Senator from Wisconsin became his greatest trial, harassing the administration at every turn with the same savage disregard for truth and justice that he had shown when his party was in opposition. The Republicans had used McCarthy as a convenient stick to beat the Democratic dog.

McCarthy had gone a long way on charges that were shown to have been almost entirely false, and to think that

Excerpted from *Eisenhower: Captive Hero—A Critical Study of the General and the President*, by Marquis Childs (New York: Harcourt, Brace, and Company, 1958). Copyright © 1958 by Marquis Childs, renewed 1986 by Marquis Childs. Reprinted by permission of Brandt & Hochman Literary Agents, Inc.

he would now reform and suddenly become a responsible member of the majority was indeed naïve. Intoxicated with the power that he had usurped, as chairman of the Senate's Government Operations Committee and the Permanent Subcommittee on Investigations, McCarthy began to assault the executive branch of the government more recklessly than ever before.

Eisenhower in Distress

How much this wild foray cost the President, his administration, and the country it is still too early to say. Accustomed to obedience from subordinates in the chain of command and utterly unfamiliar with the deeper currents of American politics, Eisenhower suffered greatly under the McCarthy goad. He has all his life been quick to anger, and the frustrations and irritations of the presidency, McCarthyism foremost among them, again and again aroused him to fury. The effect on his blood pressure and on the general condition of his health hardly needs to be pointed out. His distress was often visible in press conferences. A question on McCarthy and what he intended to do about the Senator's depredations would cause him to flush and look tense.

He had brought to his high office a civics-textbook concept of the co-ordinate powers of the three branches of the federal government. Under this concept, the executive, the legislature, and the judiciary each kept within its constitutional domain, and the government achieved thereby a neat tripartite balance. As he said in several early cabinet meetings, he intended to play by these rules, and he hoped Congress would too. If the new administration failed to act in cleaning out Communism and corruption, then, but not until then, it would be appropriate for congressional committees to investigate. This textbook approach largely left out the need for the Chief Executive to provide vigorous and positive leadership. And, as in the case of Senator Mc-

Carthy, Congress may not play by the textbook rules.

In his early responses to questions about the Senator, the President stressed his belief in the right of Congress to investigate, a right with which the executive branch could not interfere. But as McCarthy encroached with increasing directness on the Eisenhower administration itself, ignoring the effort to placate him by an extension of the federal security system that had been introduced under President Truman, these responses were scarcely adequate.

Staying Out of the Gutter

With the strain he was under more and more painfully evident, the President insisted each time that he would not deal in personalities. His angry private version of this stand, Donovan reports, was that he would "not get in the gutter" with McCarthy. In July 1953, he said he had to remind reporters again that he never dealt "in terms of personality." If a democracy, with all of its different viewpoints and approaches, was going to make progress "someone had to take on the onerous job of trying to search out, analyze and bring together the majority of view or what you might call the bulk of public opinion. . . . You could not get ahead merely by indulging in extremist views and listening to them. . . ." Asked in November whether he thought Communists-in-government would be an issue in the next election, he replied that he hoped it would be a matter of history and memory by then. He didn't believe we could live in fear of each other forever, and he really hoped and believed that this administration was "proceeding decently and justly to get this thing straightened out." But he again acknowledged Congress's right to investigate and said he saw no reason for expressing his "personal opinion" on congressional activities unless it seemed "necessary . . . to the welfare of the country."

A valid argument could be made that the President was taking the wise course in avoiding a personal dispute with

McCarthy. So confident was the Senator of his prowess at this point that he would have liked to engage the President of the United States in a public battle. Those close to the President argued that this would only serve to increase McCarthy's stature. The dominant belief in the White House was that McCarthy would destroy himself, with public opinion eventually turning against him for his excesses. For the President to contend with him would merely prolong the evil.

The Damage McCarthyism Caused

While this sounded plausible enough, it conveniently ignored the grave damage daily being done by McCarthyism. This damage was compounded by the fact that the administration apparently felt no responsibility for coming to the rescue of innocent victims of McCarthy in government. When Harold Stassen ventured to criticize McCarthy for his "negotiations" with Greek shipowners on trade with Communist countries, the President repudiated Stassen's remarks. Secretary of State Dulles conferred with McCarthy and, in Donovan's words, "assured the senator that he had acted in the national interest. . . ." Victim after victim was sacrificed by summary dismissal from government. The demoralization in the Foreign Service and the Voice of America could hardly be exaggerated.

The damage done by the McCarthy obsession was perhaps greatest in the field of foreign relations. When the incredible [McCarthy aides Roy] Cohn and [David] Schine were let loose on Europe it seemed that some kind of limit of insanity had been reached. Flying from capital to capital, they intimidated responsible officials, ordered books taken out of USIA [United States Information Agency] libraries, and generally behaved, as the European press duly noted, like two irresponsible juveniles turned loose with political tommy guns. It was not merely that the whole apparatus for conducting foreign relations suffered grave impairment.

This went so far that five senior retired diplomats of impeccable reputation and great distinction felt called upon to make a public protest. But throughout the world our prestige was damaged as our friends laughed in embarrassment, hoping that the seizure was only temporary, while our enemies jeered and made the utmost use in propaganda of the whole McCarthy madness.

While the effect of the damage in this field is still incalculable, in scientific research and development the toll was also very high. The work of the important electronics research center at Fort Monmouth was seriously disrupted when McCarthy and his agents rode through shooting at everything that moved. As the security system became more extensive and more rigorous in response to the McCarthy hysteria, scientists became reluctant to commit themselves to the security straitjacket. Accustomed to freedom of inquiry and the free exchange of information, they preferred more often than not to avoid government research or even research conducted by private agencies under government sponsorship. These were the intellectuals, the long-haired academic men of whom the President had spoken in South Dakota with implied scorn. In the same vein, Postmaster General Summerfield's boast of Republican "progress in rooting out the eggheads" and Eisenhower's 1954 definition of an intellectual as "a man who takes more words than necessary to tell us more than he knows" were hardly calculated to add to the allure of federal employment among scholars and scientists. And when it came to rewards, industry was competing for their services with far more generous salary offers.

Almost no one took note at the time of what this might cost the nation in the contest with the Soviet Union for the lead in scientific and technological development. In retrospect, it seems to have been taken for granted that the United States would inevitably maintain this lead no matter what we did or did not do. Administration orators rarely failed to claim the inevitable superiority in all departments of the free world over totalitarian dictatorship. One of the few who did express concern on this score was Dr. James R. Killian, president of Massachusetts Institute of Technology and later to be President Eisenhower's special co-ordinator of science and research. Testifying before a House committee in 1954, Killian reported that scientists were "discouraged and apprehensive" about "what sometimes seems a preoccupation with security procedures and policies at the expense of scientific progress." He stated his belief "that the whole problem of security procedures and policies at the present time may be one of the things that is most hazardous to our future research and development activity in this country in relation to military problems."

Eisenhower Silent

Yet for all the harm that was being done in a variety of fields, and the evidence was repeatedly made plain, the record shows that virtually no one in authority spoke out in protest. The President, in his speech at Dartmouth College in 1953, did put in an extemporaneous reference to the evils of book burning, prompted by his friend John J. McCloy, who sat on the platform with him. At a subsequent press conference, however, he largely nullified the effect of this warning. It must be said in his defense that his party in Congress was deeply divided. Senator McCarthy had an important following, and Senator Bricker, with his amendment to restrict the treaty-making powers of the chief executive, caused the President as much unhappiness and worry as any single element in the first two years. Only by the vote of one Democrat, who came onto the Senate floor at the last moment, was the Bricker amendment, which the President had said would make the conduct of foreign policy impossible, defeated.

CHAPTER

4

SCHOOL

DESEGREGATION

Eisenhower Against the *Brown v. Board* Decision

James T. Patterson

Although Eisenhower was responsible for selecting Earl Warren to be Chief Justice of the U.S. Supreme Court, he did not agree with the opinion of that court in *Brown v. Board of Education of Topeka, Kansas*, the Warren court's most famous decision. In *Brown v. Board* the Court ruled unanimously that the doctrine of "separate but equal" was unconstitutional, and therefore segregated schools were illegal. The ruling was welcomed by African Americans and proponents of the civil rights movement, but was opposed by many Southern whites. Eisenhower himself declared that he would support the Supreme Court, but did not agree with the ruling, arguing that the Court's actions would lead to greater conflict between supporters and critics of desegregation. In this essay, James T. Patterson, a professor of history at Brown University, argues that Eisenhower's reputation and moral authority as president were so great that he could—and should—have united the country behind the *Brown* decision.

SUPPORTERS OF *BROWN* IN 1954–55 ESPECIALLY YEARNED for backing from the most commanding white leader of all: President Eisenhower. Ike enjoyed enormous public

Excerpted from *Brown v. Board of Education: A Civil Rights Milestone and Its Troubled Legacy*, by James T. Patterson (New York: Oxford University Press, 2001). Copyright © 2001 by James T. Patterson. Reprinted with permission.

standing and popularity at the time. Many white business leaders in the South, who were keys to community responses to *Brown*, especially admired him. So did many influential southern whites who had served in the armed forces. If Eisenhower were to speak out strongly for the decision, other whites would presumably have to listen. If he chastised obstructionists [those who opposed desegragation], they, too, might back down a bit.

Eisenhower Saw Himself as Racially Tolerant

Eisenhower, like millions of white Americans at the time, considered himself a racially tolerant man. As president he issued executive orders desegregating federal facilities such as shipyards and veterans' hospitals. He encouraged the desegregation of public schools in the District of Columbia. His liberal attorney general, Herbert Brownell, supported the Fund's efforts. In his second term, Eisenhower signed two civil rights bills. Both the bills were weak and had little effect; still, they were the first to get through Congress since the days of Reconstruction following the Civil War.

But—again like most white Americans—Eisenhower had grown up in a virtually all-white world. There had been no blacks in his hometown in Kansas or in his class at West Point. He had spent much of his adult life in a Jim Crow army and had opposed as disruptive [President Harry] Truman's order to desegregate the armed services in 1948. He had many friends in the South who were outspoken about the incompetence, as they saw it, of their "darkies," and who adamantly supported racial segregation.

A Cautious Approach

Eisenhower approached the issue of school desegregation very cautiously. Some of his top advisers, noting the gains the Republican party had made among white voters in the South during the 1952 election, urged him to move carefully lest the party forfeit possible political advantage. More important, the president was philosophically conservative about the capacity of government to change the hearts and minds of people. "The improvement of race relations," he wrote in his diary in 1953, "is one of those things that will be healthy and sound only if it starts locally. I do not believe that prejudices . . . will succumb to compulsion. Consequently, I believe that Federal law imposed upon our States . . . would set back the cause of race relations a long, long time." He wrote the daughter of [African American activist] Booker T. Washington, "We cannot do it [improve race relations] by cold lawmaking, but must make these changes by appealing to reason, by prayer, and by constantly working at it through our own efforts."

If Earl Warren had any uncertainties about the president's attitude on such matters, they were probably resolved while the Court was considering *Brown* in early 1954. At that time Eisenhower invited him to a dinner at the White House and sat him next to John W. Davis, who was leading the defense team against [National Association for the Advancement of Colored People (NAACP) legal director Thurgood] Marshall. After telling Warren that Davis was a great American, Eisenhower took the Chief Justice by the arm and explained to him the southern point of view. Southern whites, he said, "are not bad people. All they are concerned about is to see that their sweet little girls are not required to sit in school alongside some big overgrown Negro."

When the Court announced *Brown* shortly thereafter, Eisenhower was unhappy. When reporters demanded to know his opinion of the decision, he responded that he was duty-bound as president to accept it. But he refused to endorse it. "The Supreme Court has spoken," he said awkwardly, "and I am sworn to uphold their—the constitutional processes in this country, and I am trying. I will obey." There was no doubting, however, his private feelings. He told a speechwriter,

I am convinced that the Supreme Court decision set back progress in the South at least fifteen years. . . . It's all very well to talk about school integration—if you remember that you may also be talking about social disintegration. Feelings are deep on this, especially where children are involved. . . . We can't demand perfection in these moral things. All we can do is keep working toward a goal and keep it high. And the fellow who tries to tell me that you can do these things by FORCE is just plain NUTS.

Eisenhower Should Have Supported *Brown v. Board*

When Eisenhower said that "feelings run deep" on the issue, he surely meant his own feelings in particular. Neither then nor at any time during the remaining years of his presidency did he endorse the *Brown* decision. In the 1956 campaign, he (like his Democratic opponent, Adlai Stevenson) stated that he could "not imagine any set of circumstances" that would lead him to send in federal troops to enforce court orders for desegregation. When a crisis over desegregating schools in Little Rock [Arkansas] erupted a year later, he had to eat his words, but defended his action as needed to preserve order, not to liberalize race relations. As Commander in Chief he had a duty to prevent violence.

Eisenhower's decidedly cool approach to desegregation of the races was hardly unusual in 1954. After all, most white Northerners at the time were equally cool. And white Southerners did have "feelings" that "ran deep." But the president, an extraordinarily popular figure, could have used the White House as a "bully pulpit." His refusal to do so was morally obtuse, and it allowed Southern intransigence—except in the case of Little Rock in 1957—to go unchallenged. With reason, it deeply angered advocates of civil rights. Roy Wilkins, executive secretary of the NAACP, exclaimed, "If he had fought World War II the way he fought for civil rights, we would all be speaking German today."

"I Will Obey": Eisenhower and *Brown v. Board*

Peter Lyon

After the death of Supreme Court Chief Justice Fred Vinson on September 8, 1953, Eisenhower appointed Earl Warren to the vacant seat. In making the appointment Eisenhower was trying—as always—to steer a middle course between the extreme left and the extreme right in American politics. Soon after his appointment, however, Warren presided over the *Brown v. Board* decision to abolish segregation in public schools. In this excerpt from *Eisenhower: Portrait of the Hero*, Peter Lyon argues that Eisenhower was shocked and infuriated by the *Brown v. Board* decision, and especially by the rapid polarization of a figure he had seen as a true centrist on the Court. Despite his great anger, Lyon points out, Eisenhower responded appropriately to the orders of the Supreme Court. "The Supreme Court has spoken," Eisenhower explained, "and I am sworn to uphold the constitutional processes in this country; and I will obey." Lyon has written several books, including *The UN In Action* and *The Wild, Wild West.*

I N ABILENE, WHEN EISENHOWER WAS GROWING UP THERE, HE used to play black man, or crack the whip, or shinny. "Our games at that time always seemed to involve running," his brother Edgar said later. "It is only a happy boy

Excerpted from *Eisenhower: Portrait of the Hero*, by Peter Lyon (Boston: Little, Brown and Company, 1974). Copyright © 1974 by Peter Lyon. Reprinted with permission.

that does those things." None of the children who happily played black man was a Negro, though, for no Negro families lived in Abilene. Likewise when he went to West Point, Eisenhower found himself amid white men exclusively; then and in the years that followed, the friendships he formed were with southern officers, and he slipped easily into their habits of speech and thought. Thus in a letter to his son, sent from North Africa in February 1943, he would write: "I . . . find myself living in a comfortable house, nicely heated, and staffed by Mickey [McKeogh] and a group of darkies that take gorgeous care of me." (The term "darky" was one specifically proscribed in a War Department booklet issued in 1942 to help officers command their troops more effectively.) Nevertheless, in Britain, in North Africa, and later in France, Eisenhower was at pains to ensure that the treatment of Negro troops and white troops was evenhanded. When the Allies needed tens of thousands of riflemen to carry out Eisenhower's plan for a major counterattack in the Ardennes, it was suggested that Eisenhower invite the Negro troops in the supply services to volunteer for the infantry and fight in the same command with white troops. He agreed. He had a circular drafted in which he pledged Negro volunteers they would be assigned for service in infantry units without regard to color or race. Beetle Smith, [Eisenhower's Chief of Staff during World War II] when he saw the circular, at once sent Eisenhower a sharp note characterizing it as "most dangerous . . . in regard to negro relations" and in violation of the War Department policy of segregating blacks from white troops. Eisenhower conceded that he would prefer not to "run counter to regs in a time like this" and personally rewrote the circular (Negro volunteers were segregated into platoons commanded by white officers and white noncoms). In April 1948, while Eisenhower was president at Columbia and also serving as occasional chairman of the Joint Chiefs of Staff, he was invited to testify before the

Senate Committee on the Armed Services on a bill calling for both a military draft and universal military training. Eisenhower supported both proposals, but the senators took him afield in their questioning. They wanted his views on segregation in the army and what the army was doing about it. He recommended all-Negro platoons within larger white formations. ". . . If you make a complete amalgamation," he said, "the Negro is going to be relegated to the minor jobs, and he is never going to get his promotion . . . because the competition is too tough." A regional conference of the NAACP was in session at the time, and the delegates reacted promptly and angrily. Their resolution charged Eisenhower with virtually endorsing racial segregation.

In short, like the vast majority of Americans, Dwight Eisenhower was a man who had lived most of his life almost completely insulated from his black fellow citizens; his prejudices about Negroes, like those of most white Americans, were rooted more in intellectual laziness than in positive conviction; unlike most Americans, Dwight Eisenhower was goaded by conscience to give play to his best impulses, and those impulses, nourished by the religious training of his childhood and youth, were sturdy. . . .

The Warren Court

On September 8 [1953] the chief justice of the Supreme Court, Fred Vinson, died suddenly of a heart attack, and within three weeks Eisenhower had appointed Governor Earl Warren of California in his stead.

The choice provoked a mixed reaction, one that can best be suggested by the fact that Eisenhower's brother Edgar assailed the appointment as a surrender to the Left while Eisenhower's brother Milton reported he had heard Warren was the nominee of reactionaries. To Edgar the President wrote: "From the very beginning of my acquaintanceship with [Warren], I had him in mind for an appointment to the high court—although, of course, I never anticipated an early vacancy in the chief justice position. . . . Well—here is a man of national stature, of unimpeachable integrity, of middle-of-the-road views, and with a splendid record during his years in active law work." To Milton the President wrote that Warren was "very definitely a liberal-conservative; he represents the kind of political, economic, and social thinking that I believe we need on the Supreme Court." It was absurd, he added, to think that reactionaries had recommended him.

The President was dismayed by the mixed reception and also by the rumors that came to him that he was simply paying off a political debt. If those rumors had reached him, he knew, they must also have reached Warren and so have robbed the prospective chief justice of his joy in the occasion. Eisenhower let off steam by dictating a memorandum to be entered in his private diary. He had, he said, at once ruled Dewey out of consideration for the post both because he was too political and because he was obviously Eisenhower's political sponsor. But there was "no possibility of charging that [Warren's] appointment was made as payment for a political debt," since Warren had not released his delegates at the national convention until after Eisenhower's nomination had been a certainty. Eisenhower believed Warren would "restore the prestige of the Court." Moreover, he pledged that when Warren's confirmation came up before the Senate in January: "If the Republicans as a body should try to repudiate him, I shall leave the Republican Party and try to organize an intelligent group of Independents, no matter how small."

Warren's recess appointment enabled him to join the court immediately and take part in the work of the autumn session. In November the attorney general filed a brief amicus curiae, as he had been requested to do; he argued strongly that the Fourteenth Amendment forbade racial segregation in public schools and that the Supreme Court was empowered to resolve the issue; in December an assistant attorney general, J. Lee Rankin, joined lawyers of the NAACP [National Association for the Advancement of Colored People] to argue the case before the court.

In January 1954 Eisenhower sent Warren's nomination to the Senate. For several weeks it was delayed in the Committee on the Judiciary; it was confirmed on March 1 by a voice vote without opposition.

Brown vs. Board

The chief justice sent the President a note on March 19 to express his thanks for the appointment. Four days later the President replied warmly, in his own hand. "I congratulate the nation," he wrote, "which is so fortunate as to have such a dedicated, able and devoted public servant." And week after week, on "decision Monday," the press room of the Supreme Court building filled with larger numbers of reporters awaiting an opinion in the case of *Brown vs. Board of Education of Topeka, Kansas* and associated cases involving the public school systems of Delaware, South Carolina, Virginia, and the District of Columbia. For fifty-eight years the rule of law had been that the Fourteenth Amendment was not violated if Negro children were provided "separate but equal" facilities for education; on the basis of that rule seventeen southern and border states (and the District of Columbia) had compelled segregation in their public school systems, while four others (Kansas was one) had permitted segregation.

On Monday, May 17, 1954, it was clear that something extraordinary was afoot. Rather than being told to wait for the court's opinions to be handed them in the press room, as was the custom, the reporters were ushered into the august marble court chamber to hear an opinion read by the chief justice himself, "in a firm, clear voice and with expression." The lofty hall was hushed, the audience tense, as the chief justice approached the nub of the court's unanimous opinion. "We come then," he said, "to the question presented: Does segregation of children in public schools solely on the basis of race, even though the physical facilities and other 'tangible' factors may be equal, deprive the children of the minority group of equal educational opportunities?" An infinitesimal pause. "We believe," said the chief justice, "that it does." One of the reporters present, I.F. Stone, wrote that it "was all one could do to keep from cheering, and a few of us were moved to tears." Stone singled out one sentence from the lengthy opinion. "To separate them [Negro children]," said the chief justice, "from others of a similar age and qualifications solely because of their race generates a feeling of inferiority as to their status in the community that may affect their hearts and minds in a way unlikely ever to be undone." Specifically, as to the fifty-eight-year-old rule of law, the court decreed: "Separate educational facilities are inherently unequal . . . segregation is a denial of the equal protection of the laws."

Reversal of the rule of law stunned most of the politicians and newspaper editors of the South. Reversal stunned President Eisenhower, too. He had sworn to uphold the Constitution, and he recognized that the justices of the Supreme Court were the acknowledged interpreters of the Constitution, and he could never forget that the chief justice was his man, and yet—he personally thought the decision was wrong, and he was not persuaded by the reasoning that had convinced the nine justices of the Supreme Court. Before long he would be characterizing his nomination of Earl Warren as "the biggest damnfool mistake I ever made," a more abrupt turnabout than was usual even for Eisenhower. His immediate reaction was glum. The day after the court's astonishing decision he summoned the commissioners of the District of Columbia to the White House and urged them to see to it that Washington set an example for the rest of the country in the integration of the pupils in public schools. A day later, to the reporters at his press conference, he said simply: "The Supreme Court has spoken and I am sworn to uphold the constitutional processes in this country; and I will obey."

The soldier had been given his orders. Whether he approved them or not was irrelevant. He would obey.

A Presidential Responsibility: Enforcing Order in Little Rock

Chester J. Pach Jr. and Elmo Richardson

In September 1956 Eisenhower found himself faced with a serious dilemma: Should he dispatch federal troops to keep order in Little Rock, a city seething with controversy over desegregation? Eisenhower was personally troubled by the *Brown v. Board* ruling and refused to endorse it publicly. At the same time, he was deeply committed to preserving the force of law in American society, and was infuriated that many segregationists had defied a Supreme Court ruling. In this excerpt from *The Presidency of Dwight D. Eisenhower*, Chester J. Pach Jr. and Elmo Richardson argue that Eisenhower sent troops to Little Rock more to maintain order and respect for the rulings of the Supreme Court than to make a statement about the correctness of desegregation. While Eisenhower was forced to take a public stance against the segregationists, the president himself acted instead to uphold the authority of the judicial branch of the United States government.

    Chester J. Pach Jr. is a professor of history at Ohio University. He is the author of numerous books and articles on U.S. foreign policy, including *Arming the Free World: The Origins of the United States Military Assistance Program, 1945–1950* and *The First Television War: TV News, the White House and Viet-*

Excerpted from *The Presidency of Dwight D. Eisenhower*, by Chester J. Pach Jr. and Elmo Richardson (Lawrence: University Press of Kansas, 1991). Copyright © 1991 by University Press of Kansas. All rights reserved. Reprinted with permission.

nam. Elmo Richardson is the author of several books and articles on U.S. environmental history, including *Dams, Parks, and Politics: Resource Development and Preservation in the Truman-Eisenhower Era.*

A POPULIST DEMOCRAT, [ARKANSAS GOVERNOR ORVAL] Faubus appeared to be a moderate among southern governors on race relations. Actually he was an opportunist. During his first gubernatorial campaign in 1954, he declared that Arkansas was "not ready for a complete and sudden mixing of the races in the public schools," but later pledged to use his powers as governor to carry out the decisions of local school boards. Two years later, the local authorities in Little Rock, the state capital, devised a plan for the voluntary, phased integration of their schools over seven years. The federal district court approved the plan and ordered that it begin in September 1957 at all-white Central High School. Despite his earlier promise, Faubus tried to block the desegregation of Little Rock classrooms. Even though he praised the Little Rock plan in private conversation, he publicly sided with rabid segregationists who warned that the integration of Central High School would precipitate violence. Faubus reckoned that if he did not go along with the defenders of Jim Crow, he would destroy his chances for reelection in 1958. Thus he appealed to the court to postpone the admission of blacks to Central High School in the interest of preserving public order. When federal judge Ronald Davies rejected the governor's plea, Faubus called the national guard to active duty and ordered it to prevent blacks from entering Central High School.

Having defied federal authority, Faubus took the remarkable step of seeking presidential sanction. He sent a panicked telegram to Eisenhower at the vacation White House in Newport, Rhode Island, asking for the president's help because, he alleged, the Justice Department had tapped his telephone and was preparing to arrest him. Eisenhower brusquely dismissed those charges. He advised Faubus, however, that the attorney general was looking into the crisis in Little Rock and that he would defend the Constitution "by every legal means at my command." Eisenhower certainly was upset with Faubus for causing a showdown between state and federal authority. Yet he apparently held Davies accountable as well, since he blamed the problems in Little Rock on those "people who believe you are going to reform the human heart by law."

Defusing the Crisis

Against this backdrop of mutual suspicion, Eisenhower and Faubus arranged a meeting to defuse the crisis. Acting as the governor's emissary, Arkansas Representative Brooks Hays stated that Faubus had gotten into a more complicated situation than he had expected and wanted to find some way to extricate himself. [Attorney General Herbert] Brownell advised Eisenhower that Faubus had caused his own problems and that the federal court ought to hold the governor accountable for his actions. Eisenhower, however, still hoped for a negotiated solution. At the same time, he did not want to appear to be interfering in the proper exercise of a governor's responsibilities. To resolve these difficulties, Sherman Adams, Eisenhower's chief of staff, and Hays drafted a message for Faubus to send to Eisenhower requesting a meeting. Adams insisted that Faubus declare that he intended to obey the court's order. Faubus apparently acceded to this precondition but then dispatched a telegram that contained qualifying language that Adams had not cleared. Nonetheless, Eisenhower agreed to talk to Faubus at Newport.

On 14 September, Eisenhower and Faubus seemed to settle their differences. While meeting alone with the president for fifteen minutes, Faubus repeatedly stressed that he deeply respected the rule of law and acknowledged the supremacy of federal authority. Eisenhower sympathetically assured Faubus that he did not want to see him humiliated and suggested an honorable way out of his predicament. Rather than go home and withdraw the national guard, which might make the governor appear to be backing down under pressure, Faubus should simply change the troops' orders so that they were instructed to maintain peace while the black students attended Central High School. Such action would avoid a test of strength in which "there could be only one outcome." Hays and Adams then joined the conversation followed by Brownell and Press Secretary James C. Hagerty. When the meeting adjourned after two hours, Eisenhower definitely thought Faubus had agreed to his terms.

Both of the principals issued statements, which in retrospect indicate that the deal Eisenhower thought he had made was by no means solid. Faubus described the meeting as friendly and worthwhile and indicated his "*desire* to cooperate" with Eisenhower "in carrying out the duties resting upon both of us under the Federal Constitution." He added somewhat ominously that in meeting these obligations, "the complexities of integration [must] be patiently understood by all those in federal authority." Eisenhower, for his part, said Faubus "stated his *intention* to respect the decisions of the . . . District Court and to give his full cooperation in carrying out his responsibilities in respect to these decisions." Eisenhower also stressed "the inescapable responsibility resting upon the Governor to preserve law and order in his state."

Faubus Retreats

After returning to Little Rock, Faubus temporized. He did not change the orders of the national guard, and he demanded a delay in the admission of the black students. After Judge Davies issued an injunction on 20 September that prohibited Faubus from doing anything more to stop the integration of Central High School, the governor announced the withdrawal of the national guard. He then departed for the Southern Governors' Conference in Georgia. Eisenhower prematurely breathed a sigh of relief.

Eisenhower's aides were not so sanguine. Gen. Andrew J. Goodpaster, the president's staff secretary, informed his chief that the federal government had an obligation to

Eisenhower Sends Federal Troops to Little Rock

On September 24, 1957, Eisenhower issued an executive order calling for federalization of the Arkansas National Guard and authorizing the use of federal armed forces to deal with the Little Rock school integration situation.

Whereas, certain persons in the state of Arkansas, individually and in unlawful assemblages, combinations and conspiracies, have willfully obstructed the enforcement of orders of the United States District Court for the Eastern District of Arkansas with respect to matters relating to enrollment and attendance at public schools, particularly at Central High School, located in Little Rock School District, Little Rock, Ark., and

Whereas, such willful obstruction of justice hinders the execution of the laws of that state and of the United States, and makes it impracticable to enforce such laws by the ordinary course of judicial proceedings, and

Whereas, such obstruction of justice constitutes a denial of the equal protection of the law; secured by the Constitution of the United States and impedes the court of justice under those laws:

Now, therefore, I, Dwight D. Eisenhower, president of the United States, under and by the virtue of the authority vested in me by the Constitution and statutes of the United States . . . do command all persons engaged in such ob-

make Faubus obey the court "by whatever means may be necessary." Brownell also worried that federal intervention might be necessary, especially since Faubus washed his hands of further responsibility for maintaining law and order in Little Rock when he left for Georgia. But the attorney general knew that neither federal marshals nor local police would be able to handle a civil disturbance in Little

struction of justice to cease and desist therefrom, and to disperse forthwith. . . .

Section 1. I hereby authorize and direct the secretary of defense to order into the active military service of the United States as he may deem appropriate to carry out the purposes of this order, any or all of the units of the National Guard of the United States and of the Air National Guard of the United States within the state of Arkansas to serve in the active military service of the United States for an indefinite period and until relieved by appropriate order.

Section 2. The secretary of defense is authorized and directed to take all appropriate steps to enforce any order of the United States District Court for the Eastern District of Arkansas for the removal of obstruction of justice in the state of Arkansas with respect to matters relating to enrollment and attendance at public schools in the Little Rock School District, Little Rock, Arkansas. In carrying out the provisions of this section, the secretary of defense is authorized to use the units and members thereof, ordered into active military service of the United States pursuant to Section 1 of this order.

Section 3. In furtherance of the enforcement of the aforementioned order of the United States District Court for the Eastern District of Arkansas, the secretary of defense is authorized to use such of the armed forces of the United States as he may deem necessary.

Dwight Eisenhower's executive order reprinted from the *Arkansas Democrat*, September 24, 1957.

Rock. Eisenhower remarked that he was loath to send in troops because their very presence might cause violence to spread. He spent an impatient weekend wondering what would happen and uncertain about what he would do.

On Monday morning, 23 September, Little Rock erupted, much to Eisenhower's disgust. A frenzied mob of more than a thousand people, many from outside Little Rock, gathered outside Central High School to prevent its integration. "Niggers, keep away from our school," the crowd clamored. "Go back to the jungle." Just before the start of classes, some of the demonstrators attacked four black journalists, whom they apparently mistook for the parents of the students. One of the reporters, Alex Wilson, was hit in the head with a brick and "went down like a tree," according to one observer. The nine black students managed to enter unmolested through a side door. "Oh, my God, they're in the school," someone shrieked. Because the mob was so persistent and menacing, the nine black students were sent home at noontime for their own safety. Eisenhower denounced the "disgraceful" behavior of a "mob of extremists" and warned that he would use "whatever force may be necessary . . . to carry out the orders of the Federal Court." He concluded, "It will be a sad day for this country—both at home and abroad—if school children can safely attend their classes only under the protection of armed guards."

Federal Intervention

That sad day arrived only a few hours later. Once again a threatening crowd assembled near Central High School on 24 September. "People are converging on the scene from all directions," Mayor Woodrow Wilson Mann telegraphed Eisenhower. "Situation [is] out of control and police cannot disperse the mob. I am pleading with you as President of the United States . . . to provide the necessary troops within several hours." Eisenhower responded quickly. He authorized Gen. Maxwell D. Taylor, the army chief of staff, to dispatch 1,000 paratroopers from the 101st Airborne Division to Little Rock. Eisenhower wanted such a display of force that no demonstrators would dare to challenge the troops. He also federalized the Arkansas National Guard but did not want them deployed near the high school because, as he later explained, "I didn't want to have brothers fighting up against brothers and families divided." By nightfall, the troops had begun to police Little Rock. The next morning, newspapers carried shocking pictures of the troops patrolling with fixed bayonets. A few editors provided acid commentary by juxtaposing these photographs with pictures of Eisenhower playing golf at Newport.

After returning to Washington from Newport, Eisenhower sadly told a nationwide radio and television audience that he had sent the army into Little Rock only because of his "inescapable" responsibility to enforce the law. He laid the blame for the strife on "disorderly mobs" led by "demagogic extremists." As usual, he avoided discussion of personalities and did not even make reference to Faubus. He tried hard to make clear that the soldiers were in Little Rock not to promote integration, but to guarantee obedience to the law. Again he refused to endorse the *Brown* ruling. "Our personal opinions about the decision have no bearing on the matter of enforcement," he reminded his audience. The Supreme Court alone had the authority to interpret the Constitution, and disobedience of its rulings could lead to "anarchy." Eisenhower lamented the way in which the disorder in Arkansas had damaged the nation's image in the eyes of the world and had bolstered Communist propaganda efforts. "Our enemies are gloating over this incident and using it everywhere to misrepresent our whole nation," he reminded the American people. "We are portrayed as a violator of those standards of conduct which the peoples of the world united to proclaim in the Charter of the United Nations." He coupled appeals to patriotism with conciliatory gestures toward white southerners. From personal experience, he knew "that the overwhelming majority of the people in the South . . . are of good will, united in their efforts to preserve and respect the law even when they disagree with it." Thus he pleaded with the people of Arkansas to return to their "normal habits of peace and order" so that the troops could be speedily withdrawn.

Eisenhower's handling of the Little Rock crisis was exceptional, but understandable. Absolutely central to his decision was the sense of personal betrayal he felt over Faubus's conduct. The governor had given his word and then reneged on it. Eisenhower was outraged, but far more important was his conviction that he could not trust Faubus to step in and restore order once the mobs gathered outside Central High School. Also critical was the sense of duty he felt to protect the Constitution and uphold federal law. Despite his own reservations about the *Brown* ruling, he could not turn his back on a mob that tried to substitute its will for that of a federal judge. "If the day comes when we can obey the orders of our Courts only when we personally approve of them," he reminded [his childhood friend] Swede Hazlett, "the end of the American system, as we know it, will not be far off." Finally, Eisenhower had exhausted all other alternatives short of armed intervention. His negotiations with Faubus had fallen through; his public appeal to the rioters to cease and desist had been ignored. Local officials appealed to him to act. Eisenhower had to heed their call. As historian Stephen E. Ambrose has written, "He could not have done otherwise and still been President."

A Gloom over the Presidency

Herbert S. Parmet

The American public initially approved of Eisenhower's decision to send federal troops to Little Rock, Arkansas. The positive poll numbers, however, served to mask a serious problem for the Republican party. In this excerpt from *Eisenhower and the American Crusades*, Herbert S. Parmet argues that Eisenhower's decision destroyed Republican hopes of attracting Southern voters and ultimately resulted in a serious decline in the president's popularity. Eisenhower, Parmet contends, expended significant GOP political capital in order to uphold *Brown v. Board of Education*. Parmet is a professor of history at the City University of New York and is the author of several works on U.S. politicians, including *Jack: The Struggles of John F. Kennedy*, *George Bush: The Life of a Lone Star Yankee*, and *Richard Nixon and His America*.

BY SEPTEMBER [1956], WITH THE END OF THE CONGRESsional battle over the Civil Rights Act of 1957, final arrangements were being made. In Newport, Rhode Island, the President signed the new law on September 9. The White House had agreed to invite a delegation that would include Roy Wilkins, A. Philip Randolph, Martin Luther King, Jr., Jackie Robinson and Dr. Frederick Douglass Patterson, the president emeritus of Tuskegee Insti-

Excerpted from *Eisenhower and the American Crusades*, by Herbert S. Parmet (New Brunswick, NJ: Transaction Publishers, 1999). Copyright © 1999 by Transaction Publishers. Reprinted with permission.

tute. One unresolved matter pertained to the site of the conference. Would it take place in Washington or at the naval base in Newport, Rhode Island, where the President had gone for a vacation?

Ironically, however, Newport became, instead, the site of another conference, one of ultimately greater importance for both the progress of racial equality in America and the exercise of the President's constitutional powers. The events leading to that session, the effective obstruction by Governor Orval Faubus of the integration of Central High School in Little Rock, Arkansas, had also killed for the duration all plans to have the President confer with the black delegation. On the same day Morrow sent a memorandum to Sherman Adams about completing arrangements for the Presidential meeting with the Negroes, Faubus wired that he would arrive at Eisenhower's vacation headquarters on Saturday, September 14.

Faubus Acts

Governor Faubus, with a reputation as a racial moderate that had, in fact, been the target of a rough primary campaign conducted by the Leader of the Arkansas White Citizens Council, had taken the first step toward permanent enshrinement in the scrolls of resistors of integration. Defying both a federal court order and its compliance by Little Rock's Board of Education, Faubus had used the state's National Guard to block the entry into the school of nine Negro students. The resistance that September 3, after integration had already been effectuated elsewhere in the state, marked a bold defiance of federal law. Unhappily for the President, Faubus had also shaken his determination to avoid implementing integration by force of arms.

As Faubus arrived at Newport on that Saturday morning, via helicopter from Providence, he had reason to believe his position would be understood. Only on July 17 Eisenhower's dislike for using federal troops was stated clearly and publicly in response to a press-conference question about the powers that would be available under the original draft of Part III of the civil-rights legislation currently being debated in Congress. "I can't imagine any set of circumstances," he declared, "that would ever induce me to send federal troops into a federal court and into any area to enforce the orders of a federal court, because I believe that [the] common sense of America will never require it."

As recently as eleven days before Faubus's arrival, hours before leaving Washington for Newport, he responded to the Governor's move by ignoring the obvious constitutional issue. He repeated, instead, his caution about the fallacies of changing "people's hearts merely by laws" and, seeming very sensitive to the sentiments behind Southern resistance, noted their strong emotional opposition to what they called the "mongrelization of the race." Additionally, what Faubus did not know but later suspected, Eisenhower and Herbert Brownell differed on whether a meeting with the Governor could be productive and, moreover, sympathized more than the Attorney General with the Governor's need to comply while retaining his newly won credentials with the segregationists. Yet, on September 5, in replying to a telegram from Faubus requesting understanding of his action and asking removal of FBI investigators from the scene, the President offered a direct reminder of his own responsibility to uphold the Constitution "by every legal means at my command."

A Personal Response

But Eisenhower's continued faith in his personal diplomacy won out. Meeting alone with the President at the naval base, Faubus stressed, as he had earlier, the rioting that had been avoided by his act and probably hoped, as Sherman Adams suspected, to convince the President to cooperate in rescinding the federal court order. The President stood by the need to comply, however, and to achieve desegregation gradually. Faubus found their conference encouraging until the conversation included Attorney General Brownell. When the Governor left Newport, he gave no hint about his ultimate course. Whether he would withdraw the National Guard remained unanswered.

The Arkansas troops remained at Central High throughout the following week. Then, after federal judge Ronald Davies ordered their removal, Faubus complied. Monday, September 23, brought the greatest turmoil since the *Brown v. Topeka* decision as an angry mob, inflated by trouble-seekers from the neighboring countryside, despite the presence of local and state police, forced the nine students from the building. That same evening the President issued a statement denouncing the "disgraceful occurrences" and warned that continued obstruction would bring out "whatever force may be necessary" to implement the court's order.

Little changed by the next morning. Mayor Woodrow Wilson Mann of Little Rock sent a frantic telegram to Newport that told the story:

> The immediate need for federal troops is urgent. The mob is much larger in numbers at 8 AM than at any time yesterday. People are converging on the scene from all directions. Mob is armed and engaging in fisticuffs and other acts of violence. Situation is out of control and police cannot disperse the mob. I am pleading to you as President of the United States in the interest of humanity law and order and because of democracy worldwide to provide the necessary federal troops within several hours. Action by you will restore peace and order and compliance with your proclamation.

Federal Force

The Constitution, the Presidency and Eisenhower had all been defied. Sherman Adams has written that his subsequent deployment of a massive force, consistent with his belief in the discreet but effective use of the military, was the most repugnant move he ever had to make as President. But, in that state of anarchy, lives were at stake and the right of children to go to school never more clearly denied before a watchful world. Thus, the circumstances he could not have imagined just a short time ago had forced him to act.

Ten thousand Arkansas National Guardsmen were nationalized, thereby giving responsibility for implementing integration to the same forces that had been turning the students back, and one thousand paratroopers from the 101st Airborne Division were also rushed into the area. All were placed under the command of Major General Edwin A. Walker, whose name, ironically, later became associated with the most extreme right-wing groups that began to emerge with the close of the Eisenhower era. The integration of Central High was consequently accomplished, but under an armed guard for the rest of the school year. After having been closed by Faubus for the 1958–1959 session, reopening came in August of 1959 under a federal court order.

Finally, after all the politic delays, Eisenhower met with four Negro leaders in the White House on June 23, 1958. Dr. King, Roy Wilkins and Lester Granger were there with A. Philip Randolph, who was their spokesman. The carefully planned conference, which lasted nearly one hour, consisted largely of having Randolph read a nine-point program that called on the President to establish a "clear national policy" against racial discrimination that would include more vigorous enforcement by the Justice Department of black rights to life, property and voting. Mostly, the President listened and seemed sympathetic. At one point he included integration as but one of many major problems. When the four leaders left and had the usual post-White House conference with the press, they reported that he had been gracious and also felt their cause had been "advanced."

But the Little Rock episode, exploding as it did during

the fall of 1957, combined with other events to throw the President and his Administration into deep gloom. On the surface, Americans polled by the Gallup people expressed approval for the President's move. Sixty-four percent said he had done the "right thing." Even many Southerners, a surprisingly high 36 percent, agreed, but mostly through the belief that inaction would have encouraged further rioting and even bloodshed. Interestingly, all regions agreed that the President had acted wisely in not sending troops any sooner. One Little Rock School Board member, in a personal note to Mr. Eisenhower, praised him for having made an appropriate response to a correct analysis of the situation. Martin Luther King, Jr., rejoiced over what he told the President was "of great benefit to our nation and to the Christian traditions of fair play and brotherhood." Indeed, thoughts about the precedent that would have been created by failure to support integration against mob rule left little question about the future importance of the President's decision.

At the same time, however, Little Rock immediately threatened to destroy whatever hopes the GOP retained of wooing the South. When the Southern Governors met at Sea Island, Georgia, for their annual conference on the day the troops moved in, they could talk about nothing else. Congressman Billy Mathews of Gainsville, Florida, complained bitterly that the South had been cheated, that Part III of the Civil Rights Act had in effect been used although its obnoxious provisions had been eliminated. The move, he wrote to the President, had "placed federal troops, our own troops, with bayonets in their hand, to enforce integration." . . .

All through the spring and summer of 1957, during the budget and civil-rights battles, and while the cost of living continued to rise and the President's personal popularity slipped from month to month, the party revolt gained momentum. "Rising population, rising prices and rising criticism are the order of the day at home," wrote James Reston. There was talk about the "erosion of the Presidency" and the discrediting of whatever was meant by "modern Republicanism." Senator George Aiken, an independent moderate, warned that the GOP belonged to Republicans and not solely to Eisenhower. Meade Alcorn, too, moving along with the rightward drift, began to describe "modern Republicanism" in ways that sounded indistinguishable from the traditional variety. He told a Nebraska audience that the "Government should be the people's servant and not their master" and then, in a speech the following month, renewed old charges that Democrats had "coddled Communists" and brought a climate for corruption. Faced with a question at his May 15 news conference about charges being made by Congressional Republicans that he had "moved somewhat to the left" since 1952, Eisenhower responded by saying, "Far from it. If anything, I think I have grown more conservative." Coincidentally, with Eisenhower's new vulnerability, rumors spread about his physical condition. He even had to refute as the "worst rot that I have heard since I have been in this office" reports that he was contemplating resigning and turning over the reigns of government to Vice President Nixon.

APPENDIX OF DOCUMENTS

Document 1: "The Future Shall Belong to the Free"

Dwight Eisenhower enumerated the guiding principles of his administration's foreign policy in his first inaugural address on Tuesday, January 20, 1953.

The world and we have passed the midway point of a century of continuing challenge. We sense with all our faculties that forces of good and evil are massed and armed and opposed as rarely before in history.

This fact defines the meaning of this day. We are summoned by this honored and historic ceremony to witness more than the act of one citizen swearing his oath of service, in the presence of God. We are called as a people to give testimony in the sight of the world to our faith that the future shall belong to the free. . . .

In pleading our just cause before the bar of history and in pressing our labor for world peace, we shall be guided by certain fixed principles.

These principles are:

(1) Abhorring war as a chosen way to balk the purposes of those who threaten us, we hold it to be the first task of statesmanship to develop the strength that will deter the forces of aggression and promote the conditions of peace. For, as it must be the supreme purpose of all free men, so it must be the dedication of their leaders, to save humanity from preying upon itself.

In the light of this principle, we stand ready to engage with any and all others in joint effort to remove the causes of mutual fear and distrust among nations, so as to make possible drastic reduction of armaments. The sole requisites for undertaking such effort are that—in their purpose—they be aimed logically and honestly toward secure peace for all; and that—in their result—they provide methods by which every participating nation will prove good faith in carrying out its pledge.

(2) Realizing that common sense and common decency alike dictate the futility of appeasement, we shall never try to placate an aggressor by the false and wicked bargain of trading honor for security. Americans, indeed all free men, remember that in the final choice

a soldier's pack is not so heavy a burden as a prisoner's chains.

(3) Knowing that only a United States that is strong and immensely productive can help defend freedom in our world, we view our Nation's strength and security as a trust upon which rests the hope of free men everywhere. It is the firm duty of each of our free citizens and of every free citizen everywhere to place the cause of his country before the comfort, the convenience of himself.

(4) Honoring the identity and the special heritage of each nation in the world, we shall never use our strength to try to impress upon another people our own cherished political and economic institutions.

(5) Assessing realistically the needs and capacities of proven friends of freedom, we shall strive to help them to achieve their own security and well-being. Likewise, we shall count upon them to assume, within the limits of their resources, their full and just burdens in the common defense of freedom.

(6) Recognizing economic health as an indispensable basis of military strength and the free world's peace, we shall strive to foster everywhere, and to practice ourselves, policies that encourage productivity and profitable trade. For the impoverishment of any single people in the world means danger to the well-being of all other peoples.

(7) Appreciating that economic need, military security and political wisdom combine to suggest regional groupings of free peoples, we hope, within the framework of the United Nations, to help strengthen such special bonds the world over. The nature of these ties must vary with the different problems of different areas.

In the Western Hemisphere, we enthusiastically join with all our neighbors in the work of perfecting a community of fraternal trust and common purpose.

In Europe, we ask that enlightened and inspired leaders of the Western nations strive with renewed vigor to make the unity of their peoples a reality. Only as free Europe unitedly marshals its strength can it effectively safeguard, even with our help, its spiritual and cultural heritage.

(8) Conceiving the defense of freedom, like freedom itself, to be one and indivisible, we hold all continents and peoples in equal regard and honor. We reject any insinuation that one race or another, one people or another, is in any sense inferior or expendable.

(9) Respecting the United Nations as the living sign of all people's hope for peace, we shall strive to make it not merely an eloquent

symbol but an effective force. And in our quest for an honorable peace, we shall neither compromise, nor tire, nor ever cease.

By these rules of conduct, we hope to be known to all peoples.

By their observance, an earth of peace may become not a vision but a fact.

This hope—this supreme aspiration—must rule the way we live.

Dwight Eisenhower, First Inaugural Address, Tuesday, January 20, 1953.

Document 2: The Chance for Peace

In his first formal address to the American people since his inauguration, Eisenhower addressed how U.S. policy differed from that of the Soviet Union.

In this spring of 1953 the free world weighs one question above all others: the chances for a just peace for all peoples.

To weigh this chance is to summon instantly to mind another recent moment of great decision. It came with that yet more hopeful spring of 1945, bright with the promise of victory and of freedom. The hopes of all just men in that moment too was a just and lasting peace.

The 8 years that have passed have seen that hope waver, grow dim, and almost die. And the shadow of fear again has darkly lengthened across the world. Today the hope of free men remains stubborn and brave, but it is sternly disciplined by experience. It shuns not only all crude counsel of despair but also the self-deceit of easy illusion. It weighs the chances for peace with sure, clear knowledge of what happened to the vain hopes of 1945.

In that spring of victory the soldiers of the Western Allies met the soldiers of Russia in the center of Europe. They were triumphant comrades in arms. Their peoples shared the joyous prospect of building, in honor of their dead, the only fitting monument—an age of just peace. All these war-weary peoples shared too this concrete, decent purpose: to guard vigilantly against the domination ever again of any part of the world by a single, unbridled aggressive power.

This common purpose lasted an instant and perished. The nations of the world divided to follow two distinct roads.

The United States and our valued friends, the other free nations, chose one road.

The leaders of the Soviet Union chose another.

The way chosen by the United States was plainly marked by a few clear precepts, which govern its conduct in world affairs.

First: No people on earth can be held, as a people, to be an enemy, for all humanity shares the common hunger for peace and fellowship and justice.

Second: No nation's security and well-being can be lastingly achieved in isolation but only in effective cooperation with fellow-nations.

Third: Every nation's right to a form of government and an economic system of its own choosing is inalienable.

Fourth: Any nation's attempt to dictate to other nations their form of government is indefensible.

And fifth: A nation's hope of lasting peace cannot be firmly based upon any race in armaments but rather upon just relations and honest understanding with all other nations.

In the light of these principles the citizens of the United States defined the way they proposed to follow, through the aftermath of war, toward true peace.

This way was faithful to the spirit that inspired the United Nations: to prohibit strife, to relieve tensions, to banish fears. This way was to control and to reduce armaments. This way was to allow all nations to devote their energies and resources to the great and good tasks of healing the war's wounds, of clothing and feeding and housing the needy, of perfecting a just political life, of enjoying the fruits of their own toil.

The Soviet government held a vastly different vision of the future. In the world of its design, security was to be found, not in mutual trust and mutual aid but in force: huge armies, subversion, rule of neighbor nations. The goal was power superiority at all cost. Security was to be sought by denying it to all others.

The result has been tragic for the world and, for the Soviet Union, it has also been ironic.

The amassing of Soviet power alerted free nations to a new danger of aggression. It compelled them in self-defense to spend unprecedented money and energy for armaments. It forced them to develop weapons of war now capable of inflicting instant and terrible punishment upon any aggressor.

It instilled in the free nations—and let none doubt this—the unshakable conviction that, as long as there persists a threat to freedom, they must, at any cost, remain armed, strong, and ready for the risk of war.

It inspired them—and let none doubt this—to attain a unity of purpose and will beyond the power of propaganda or pressure to break, now or ever.

There remained, however, one thing essentially unchanged and unaffected by Soviet conduct. This unchanged thing was the readiness of the free world to welcome sincerely any genuine evidence of peaceful purpose enabling all peoples again to resume their common quest of just peace. And the free world still holds to that purpose.

The free nations, most solemnly and repeatedly, have assured the Soviet Union that their firm association has never had any aggressive purpose whatsoever. Soviet leaders, however, have seemed to persuade themselves, or tried to persuade their people, otherwise.

And so it has come to pass that the Soviet Union itself has shared and suffered the very fears it has fostered in the rest of the world.

This has been the way of life forged by 8 years of fear and force.

What can the world, or any nation in it, hope for if no turning is found on this dread road?

The worst to be feared and the best to be expected can be simply stated.

The worst is atomic war.

Dwight Eisenhower, address delivered before the American Society of Newspaper Editors, April 16, 1953.

Document 3: Atoms for Peace

In December 1953, Eisenhower spoke to the General Assembly of the United Nations to suggest that the world superpowers seek to develop peaceful uses for atomic energy.

The United States would seek more than the mere reduction or elimination of atomic materials for military purposes.

It is not enough to take this weapon out of the hands of the soldiers. It must be put into the hands of those who will know how to strip its military casing and adapt it to the arts of peace.

The United States knows that if the fearful trend of atomic military buildup can be reversed, this greatest of destructive forces can be developed into a great boon, for the benefit of all mankind.

The United States knows that peaceful power from atomic energy is no dream of the future. That capability, already proved, is here—now—today. Who can doubt, if the entire body of the world's scientists and engineers had adequate amounts of fissionable material with which to test and develop their ideas, that this capability would rapidly be transformed into universal, efficient, and economic usage.

To hasten the day when fear of the atom will begin to disappear from the minds of people, and the governments of the East and West, there are certain steps that can be taken now.

I therefore make the following proposals:

The Governments principally involved, to the extent permitted by elementary prudence, to begin now and continue to make joint contributions from their stockpiles of normal uranium and fissionable materials to an International Atomic Energy Agency. We would expect that such an agency would be set up under the aegis of the United Nations. . . .

The United States is prepared to undertake these explorations in good faith. Any partner of the United States acting in the same good faith will find the United States a not unreasonable or ungenerous associate.

Undoubtedly initial and early contributions to this plan would be small in quantity. However, the proposal has the great virtue that it can be undertaken without the irritations and mutual suspicions incident to any attempt to set up a completely acceptable system of world-wide inspection and control.

The Atomic Energy Agency could be made responsible for the impounding, storage, and protection of the contributed fissionable and other materials. The ingenuity of our scientists will provide special safe conditions under which such a bank of fissionable material can be made essentially immune to surprise seizure.

The more important responsibility of this Atomic Energy Agency would be to devise methods whereby this fissionable material would be allocated to serve the peaceful pursuits of mankind. Experts would be mobilized to apply atomic energy to the needs of agriculture, medicine, and other peaceful activities. A special purpose would be to provide abundant electrical energy in the power-starved areas of the world. Thus the contributing powers would be dedicating some of their strength to serve the needs rather than the fears of mankind.

The United States would be more than willing—it would be proud to take up with others "principally involved" the development of plans whereby such peaceful use of atomic energy would be expedited.

Of those "principally involved" the Soviet Union must, of course, be one.

I would be prepared to submit to the Congress of the United States, and with every expectation of approval, any such plan that would:

First—encourage world-wide investigation into the most effective peacetime uses of fissionable material, and with the certainty that they had all the material needed for the conduct of all experiments that were appropriate;

Second—begin to diminish the potential destructive power of the world's atomic stockpiles;

Third—allow all peoples of all nations to see that, in this enlightened age, the great powers of the earth, both of the East and of the West, are interested in human aspirations first, rather than in building up the armaments of war;

Fourth—open up a new channel for peaceful discussion, and initiate at least a new approach to the many difficult problems that must be solved in both private and public conversations, if the world is to shake off the inertia imposed by fear, and is to make positive progress toward peace.

Against the dark background of the atomic bomb, the United States does not wish merely to present strength, but also the desire and the hope for peace.

Dwight Eisenhower, address before the General Assembly of the United Nations, December 8, 1953.

Document 4: The Administration's Goals

Almost a year after taking office, Eisenhower spoke to the American public on his administration's purposes and accomplishments.

This administration believes that no American—no one group of Americans—can truly prosper unless all Americans prosper. We are one family made up of millions of Americans with the same hopes for a full and happy life. We must not become a nation divided into factions, or special groups and hostile cliques.

We believe that the slum, the out-dated highway, the poor school system, deficiencies in health protection, the loss of a job, and the fear of poverty in old age—in fact, any real injustice in the business of living—penalizes us all. And this administration is committed to help you prevent them.

"Help" is the key word of this administration and of the program it presents to the Congress this Thursday. What do we mean by help? We do not mean monuments to costly and intolerant bureaucracy. We do not mean a timid unwillingness to act. We mean service—service that is effective, service that is prompt, service that is singlemindedly devoted to solving the problem.

You make up the communities of this country, where the everlasting job of building a stronger and better America must have its roots. We will seek to give national effect to your aims and aspirations. To do so, we rely on the good sense and local knowledge of the community and will therefore decentralize administration as much as possible so that the services of Government may be closer to you and thus serve you better.

For we know that you are far more knowledgeable than Washington as to the nature of your local needs. We know also that, as the local partners in any enterprise, you will be incessantly concerned with efficiency and economy—something which we are promoting in all Federal enterprises.

I know that you have unbounded confidence in the future of America. You need only the assurance that Government will neither handcuff your enterprise nor withdraw into a smug bureaucratic indifference to the welfare of American citizens, particularly those who, through no fault of their own, are in a period of adversity.

For this administration, I give you that pledge.

So much for our beliefs and the aims and purposes of this administration. What has been accomplished in the year just past? Let me list a few of these in the briefest possible fashion:

1. The fighting and the casualties in Korea mercifully have come to an end. We can therefore take more satisfaction in other blessings of our daily life.

2. Our own defenses and those of the free world have been strengthened against Communist aggression.

3. The highest security standards are being insisted upon for those employed in Government service.

4. Requests for new appropriations have been reduced by 13 billion dollars.

5. Tax reductions which go into effect this month have been made financially feasible by substantial reductions in expenditures.

6. Strangling controls on our economy have been promptly removed.

7. The fantastic paradox of farm prices, on a toboggan slide while living costs soared skyward, has ceased.

8. The cheapening by inflation of every dollar you earn, every savings account and insurance policy you own, and every pension payment you receive has been halted.

9. The proper working relationship between the executive and legislative branches of the Federal Government has been made effective.

10. Emergency immigration legislation has been enacted.

11. A strong and consistent policy has been developed toward gaining and retaining the initiative in foreign affairs.

12. A plan to harness atomic energy to the peaceful service of mankind, and to help end the climate of suspicion and fear that excites nations to war, has been proposed to the world.

Dwight Eisenhower, radio and television address to the American public, January 4, 1954.

Document 5: On Opportunities to the Physically Handicapped

In a 1955 address Eisenhower declared his full support for extending equal opportunities to "any who may be somewhat physically different or handicapped so long as that person can be made a useful member of society."

We have a country dedicated to equality of opportunity. We make much in many Fourth of July speeches that this equality of opportunity goes to all, regardless of race, color, religion, and so on. It seems to me that we might extend it, at least within our own hearts and minds, to include: "Or to any who may be somewhat physically different or handicapped so long as that person can be made a useful member of society."

No one wants to be a ward of charity. Indeed, this word "opportunity" seems to me to contain much that means happiness for the human—opportunity to expand and to be useful, to know that he is contributing his share to the advancement of that great society of which he is a part.

I think it even goes this far: we can differentiate between a government that is based upon individual opportunity, and one that is based upon regimentation, in this way: opportunity brings that richness of productivity in which all may share. Individual initiative, harnessed together for the good of the whole, is the most productive inspiration and impulse we have.

Regimentation does nothing but distribute deficits—deficits that occur when we don't take advantage of these great impulses in the human heart and mind to produce what he can for himself and for his society.

I repeat I believe, therefore, that opportunity—individual opportunity and freedom—enriches a whole society, and regimentation merely distributes the losses that have occurred.

So it seems to me we cannot afford for one moment to neglect placing opportunity in front of all that are capable of doing anything whatsoever with it. And the mere fact that a person may be minus a limb or one of his senses, or anything else, has nothing to do with it, any more than do the other differences among humans that we conclude should not be allowed to sway us in the government that is applied to all.

I could think of no greater service that this Committee over the years has contributed to the United States than to bring to each—not only the handicapped people themselves, but to all of us—the fact that opportunity does truly belong to all. We are not going to be satisfied until it is brought to them, and they are allowed to take full advantage for their own betterment and that of our glorious country.

Dwight Eisenhower, remarks to the President's Committee on the Employment of the Physically Handicapped, May 23, 1955.

Document 6: The Price of Peace

In his second inaugural address, Eisenhower spoke of the divisive force of international communism and described the price that Americans would have to pay in their search for peace and safety.

In too much of the earth there is want, discord, danger. New forces and new nations stir and strive across the earth, with power to bring, by their fate, great good or great evil to the free world's future. From the deserts of North Africa to the islands of the South Pacific one third of all mankind has entered upon an historic struggle for a new freedom; freedom from grinding poverty. Across all continents, nearly a billion people seek, sometimes almost in desperation, for the skills and knowledge and assistance by which they may satisfy from their own resources, the material wants common to all mankind.

No nation, however old or great, escapes this tempest of change and turmoil. Some, impoverished by the recent World War, seek to restore their means of livelihood. In the heart of Europe, Germany still stands tragically divided. So is the whole continent divided. And so, too, is all the world.

The divisive force is International Communism and the power that it controls.

The designs of that power, dark in purpose, are clear in practice. It strives to seal forever the fate of those it has enslaved. It strives to break the ties that unite the free. And it strives to capture—to exploit for its own greater power—all forces of change in the world, especially the needs of the hungry and the hopes of the oppressed.

Yet the world of International Communism has itself been shaken by a fierce and mighty force: the readiness of men who love freedom to pledge their lives to that love. Through the night of their bondage, the unconquerable will of heroes has struck with the swift, sharp thrust of lightning. Budapest is no longer merely the name of a city; henceforth it is a new and shining symbol of man's yearning to be free.

Thus across all the globe there harshly blow the winds of change. And, we—though fortunate be our lot—know that we can never turn our backs to them.

We look upon this shaken earth, and we declare our firm and fixed purpose—the building of a peace with justice in a world where moral law prevails.

The building of such a peace is a bold and solemn purpose. To proclaim it is easy. To serve it will be hard. And to attain it, we must be aware of its full meaning—and ready to pay its full price.

We know clearly what we seek, and why.

We seek peace, knowing that peace is the climate of freedom. And now, as in no other age, we seek it because we have been warned, by the power of modern weapons, that peace may be the only climate possible for human life itself.

Yet this peace we seek cannot be born of fear alone: it must be rooted in the lives of nations. There must be justice, sensed and shared by all peoples, for, without justice the world can know only a tense and unstable truce. There must be law, steadily invoked and respected by all nations, for without law, the world promises only such meager justice as the pity of the strong upon the weak. But the law of which we speak, comprehending the values of freedom, affirms the equality of all nations, great and small.

Splendid as can be the blessings of such a peace, high will be its cost: in toil patiently sustained, in help honorably given, in sacrifice calmly borne.

We are called to meet the price of this peace.

To counter the threat of those who seek to rule by force, we must pay the costs of our own needed military strength, and help to build the security of others.

We must use our skills and knowledge and, at times, our substance, to help others rise from misery, however far the scene of suffering may be from our shores. For wherever in the world a people knows desperate want, there must appear at least the spark of hope, the hope of progress—or there will surely rise at last the flames of conflict.

We recognize and accept our own deep involvement in the destiny of men everywhere. We are accordingly pledged to honor, and to strive to fortify, the authority of the United Nations. For in that body rests the best hope of our age for the assertion of that law by which all nations may live in dignity.

And, beyond this general resolve, we are called to act a responsible role in the world's great concerns or conflicts—whether they touch upon the affairs of a vast region, the fate of an island in the Pacific, or the use of a canal in the Middle East. Only in respecting the hopes and cultures of others will we practice the equality of all nations. Only as we show willingness and wisdom in giving counsel—in receiving counsel—and in sharing burdens, will we wisely perform the work of peace.

For one truth must rule all we think and all we do. No people can live to itself alone. The unity of all who dwell in freedom is their only sure defense. The economic need of all nations—in mutual dependence—makes isolation an impossibility; not even America's prosperity could long survive if other nations did not also prosper. No nation can longer be a fortress, lone and strong and safe. And any people, seeking such shelter for themselves, can now build only their own prison.

Dwight Eisenhower, Second Inaugural Address, Monday, January 21, 1957.

Document 7: Federal Court Orders Must Be Upheld

In September 1957, Eisenhower was forced to explain to the nation why he had found it necessary to send federal troops to maintain order in Little Rock, Arkansas.

Whenever normal agencies prove inadequate to the task and it becomes necessary for the Executive Branch of the Federal Government to use its powers and authority to uphold Federal Courts, the President's responsibility is inescapable. In accordance with that responsibility, I have today issued an Executive Order directing the use of troops under Federal authority to aid in the execution of Federal law at Little Rock, Arkansas. This became necessary when my Proclamation of yesterday was not observed, and the obstruction of justice still continues.

It is important that the reasons for my action be understood by all our citizens. As you know, the Supreme Court of the United States has decided that separate public educational facilities for the races are inherently unequal and therefore compulsory school segregation laws are unconstitutional.

Our personal opinions about the decision have no bearing on the matter of enforcement; the responsibility and authority of the Supreme Court to interpret the Constitution are very clear. Local Federal Courts were instructed by the Supreme Court to issue such orders and decrees as might be necessary to achieve admission to public schools without regard to race—and with all deliberate speed.

During the past several years, many communities in our Southern States have instituted public school plans for gradual progress in the enrollment and attendance of school children of all races in order to bring themselves into compliance with the law of the land.

They thus demonstrated to the world that we are a nation in which laws, not men, are supreme.

I regret to say that this truth—the cornerstone of our liberties— was not observed in this instance.

It was my hope that this localized situation would be brought under control by city and State authorities. If the use of local police powers had been sufficient, our traditional method of leaving the problems in those hands would have been pursued. But when large gatherings of obstructionists made it impossible for the decrees of the Court to be carried out, both the law and the national interest demanded that the President take action. . . .

The very basis of our individual rights and freedoms rests upon the certainty that the President and the Executive Branch of Government will support and insure the carrying out of the decisions of the Federal Courts, even, when necessary with all the means at the President's command.

Unless the President did so, anarchy would result.

There would be no security for any except that which each one of us could provide for himself.

The interest of the nation in the proper fulfillment of the law's requirements cannot yield to opposition and demonstrations by some few persons.

Mob rule cannot be allowed to override the decisions of our courts. . . .

A foundation of our American way of life is our national respect for law.

In the South, as elsewhere, citizens are keenly aware of the tremendous disservice that has been done to the people of Arkansas in the eyes of the nation, and that has been done to the nation in the eyes of the world.

At a time when we face grave situations abroad because of the hatred that Communism bears toward a system of government based on human rights, it would be difficult to exaggerate the harm that is being done to the prestige and influence, and indeed to the safety, of our nation and the world.

Our enemies are gloating over this incident and using it everywhere to misrepresent our whole nation. We are portrayed as a violator of those standards of conduct which the peoples of the world united to proclaim in the Charter of the United Nations. There they affirmed "faith in fundamental human rights" and "in dignity and worth of the human person" and they did so "without distinction as to race, sex, language or religion."

And so, with deep confidence, I call upon the citizens of the State of Arkansas to assist in bringing to an immediate end all interference with the law and its processes. If resistance to the Federal Court orders ceases at once, the further presence of Federal troops will be unnecessary and the City of Little Rock will return to its normal habits of peace and order and a blot upon the fair name and high honor of our nation in the world will be removed.

Thus will be restored the image of America and of all its parts as one nation, indivisible, with liberty and justice for all.

Dwight Eisenhower, address to the American public, September 24, 1957.

Document 8: Explaining the U-2 Incident

In May 1960 the Soviet Union shot down a U-2 reconnaissance plane over Russia and captured U.S. pilot Francis Gary Powers. While the Eisenhower administration initially claimed that the United States was not using U-2s in order to spy on the USSR, it was forced to recant when Soviet premier Khrushchev produced Powers. A deeply embarrassed and irritated Eisenhower explained to the press why he felt reconnaissance flights were necessary.

I have made some notes from which I want to talk to you about this U-2 incident. A full statement about this matter has been made by the State Department, and there have been several statesmanlike remarks by leaders of both parties.

For my part, I supplement what the Secretary of State has had to say with the following four main points. After that I shall have nothing further to say—for the simple reason that I can think of nothing to add that might be useful at this time.

First point is this: the need for intelligence-gathering activities.

No one wants another Pearl Harbor. This means that we must

have knowledge of military forces and preparations around the world, especially those capable of massive surprise attack.

Secrecy in the Soviet Union makes this essential. In most of the world no large-scale attack could be prepared in secret. But in the Soviet Union there is a fetish of secrecy and concealment. This is a major cause of international tension and uneasiness today. Our deterrent must never be placed in jeopardy. The safety of the whole free world demands this.

As the Secretary of State pointed out in his recent statement, ever since the beginning of my administration I have issued directives to gather, in every feasible way, the information required to protect the United States and the free world against surprise attack and to enable them to make effective preparations for defense.

My second point: the nature of intelligence-gathering activities.

These have a special and secret character. They are, so to speak, "below the surface" activities.

They are secret because they must circumvent measures designed by other countries to protect secrecy of military preparations.

They are divorced from the regular, visible agencies of government, which stay clear of operational involvement in specific detailed activities.

These elements operate under broad directives to seek and gather intelligence short of the use of force, with operations supervised by responsible officials within this area of secret activities.

We do not use our Army, Navy, or Air Force for this purpose, first, to avoid any possibility of the use of force in connection with these activities and, second, because our military forces, for obvious reasons, cannot be given latitude under broad directives but must be kept under strict control in every detail.

These activities have their own rules and methods of concealment, which seek to mislead and obscure—just as in the Soviet allegations there are many discrepancies. For example, there is some reason to believe that the plane in question was not shot down at high altitude. The normal agencies of our Government are unaware of these specific activities or of the special efforts to conceal them.

Third point: How should we view all of this activity?

It is a distasteful but vital necessity.

We prefer and work for a different kind of world—and a different way of obtaining the information essential to confidence and effective deterrence. Open societies, in the day of present weapons, are the only answer.

This was the reason for my open-skies proposal in 1955, which I was ready instantly to put into effect, to permit aerial observation over the United States and the Soviet Union which would assure that no surprise attack was being prepared against anyone. I shall bring up the open-skies proposal again in Paris, since it is a means of ending concealment and suspicion.

My final point is that we must not be distracted from the real issues of the day by what is an incident or a symptom of the world situation today.

This incident has been given great propaganda exploitation. The emphasis given to a flight of an unarmed, nonmilitary plane can only reflect a fetish of secrecy.

The real issues are the ones we will be working on at the summit—disarmament, search for solutions affecting Germany and Berlin, and the whole range of East-West relations, including the reduction of secrecy and suspicion.

Frankly, I am hopeful that we may make progress on these great issues. This is what we mean when we speak of "working for peace."

And, as I remind you, I will have nothing further to say about this matter.

Dwight Eisenhower, news conference statement, May 11, 1960.

Document 9: Recovering from the U-2 Incident

Shortly after the capture of Francis Gary Powers, Eisenhower left for a planned summit with Soviet premier Nikita Khrushchev in Paris. On May 15, Khrushchev announced that he expected the United States to apologize for the U-2 overflights. When Eisenhower balked, Khrushchev withdrew his invitation to Eisenhower to visit the Soviet Union and also withdrew from the summit. Eisenhower's remarks on the incident are excerpted below.

Having in mind the great importance of this conference and the hopes that the peoples of all the world have reposed in this meeting, I concluded that in the circumstances it was best to see if at today's private meeting any possibility existed through the exercise of reason and restraint to dispose of this matter of the overflights, which would have permitted the conference to go forward. . . .

Accordingly, at this morning's private session, despite the violence and inaccuracy of Mr. Khrushchev's statements, I replied to him in the following terms:

In my statement of May 11th and in the statement of Secretary

Herter of May 9th the position of the United States was made clear with respect to the distasteful necessity of espionage activities in a world where nations distrust each other's intentions. We pointed out that these activities had no aggressive intent but rather were to assure the safety of the United States and the free world against surprise attack by a power which boasts of its ability to devastate the United States and other countries by missiles armed with atomic warheads. . . .

There is in the Soviet statement an evident misapprehension on one key point. It alleges that the United States has, through official statements, threatened continued overflights. The importance of this alleged threat was emphasized and repeated by Mr. Khrushchev. The United States has made no such threat. Neither I nor my Government has intended any. The actual statements go no further than to say that the United States will not shirk its responsibility to safeguard against surprise attack.

In point of fact, these flights were suspended after the recent incident and are not to be resumed. Accordingly, this cannot be the issue.

I have come to Paris to seek agreements with the Soviet Union which would eliminate the necessity for all forms of espionage, including overflights. I see no reason to use this incident to disrupt the conference.

Should it prove impossible, because of the Soviet attitude, to come to grips here in Paris with this problem and the other vital issues threatening world peace, I am planning in the near future to submit to the United Nations a proposal for the creation of a United Nations aerial surveillance to detect preparations for attack. This plan I had intended to place before this conference. This surveillance system would operate in the territories of all nations prepared to accept such inspection. For its part, the United States is prepared not only to accept United Nations aerial surveillance but to do everything in its power to contribute to the rapid organization and successful operation of such international surveillance.

We of the United States are here to consider in good faith the important problems before this conference. We are prepared either to carry this point no further or to undertake bilateral conversations between the United States and the U.S.S.R. while the main conference proceeds.

Mr. Khrushchev brushed aside all arguments of reason and not only insisted upon this ultimatum but also insisted that he was going to publish his statement in full at the time of his own choosing. It was thus made apparent that he was determined to wreck the Paris conference. . . .

In spite of this serious and adverse development I have no intention whatsoever to diminish my continuing efforts to promote progress toward a peace with Justice. This applies to the remainder of my stay in Paris as well as thereafter.

Dwight Eisenhower, summit conference statement, May 16, 1960.

Document 10: Farewell to the Nation

After eight years as president, Eisenhower gave his final address to the nation on January 17, 1961. Eisenhower thanked the American people for allowing him to serve as president, but also warned of the power of the developing military-industrial complex in the United States.

The record of many decades stands as proof that our people and their Government have, in the main, understood these truths and have responded to them well in the face of threat and stress.

But threats, new in kind or degree, constantly arise. . . .

A vital element in keeping the peace is our military establishment. Our arms must be mighty, ready for instant action, so that no potential aggressor may be tempted to risk his own destruction.

Our military organization today bears little relation to that known by any of my predecessors in peacetime, or indeed by the fighting men of World War II or Korea.

Until the latest of our world conflicts, the United States had no armaments industry. American makers of plowshares could, with time and as required, make swords as well. But now we can no longer risk emergency improvisation of national defense; we have been compelled to create a permanent armaments industry of vast proportions. Added to this, three and a half million men and women are directly engaged in the defense establishment. We annually spend on military security more than the net income of all United States corporations.

This conjunction of an immense military establishment and a large arms industry is new in the American experience. The total influence—economic, political, even spiritual—is felt in every city, every Statehouse, every office of the Federal government. We recognize the imperative need for this development. Yet we must not fail to comprehend its grave implications. Our toil, resources and livelihood are all involved; so is the very structure of our society.

In the councils of government, we must guard against the acquisition of unwarranted influence, whether sought or unsought, by the military-industrial complex. The potential for the disastrous rise of misplaced power exists and will persist.

We must never let the weight of this combination endanger our liberties or democratic processes. We should take nothing for granted. Only an alert and knowledgeable citizenry can compel the proper meshing of the huge industrial and military machinery of defense with our peaceful methods and goals, so that security and liberty may prosper together.

Akin to, and largely responsible for the sweeping changes in our industrial-military posture, has been the technological revolution during recent decades.

In this revolution, research has become central, it also becomes more formalized, complex, and costly. A steadily increasing share is conducted for, by, or at the direction of, the Federal government.

Today, the solitary inventor, tinkering in his shop, has been overshadowed by task forces of scientists in laboratories and testing fields. In the same fashion, the free university, historically the fountainhead of free ideas and scientific discovery, has experienced a revolution in the conduct of research. Partly because of the huge costs involved, a government contract becomes virtually a substitute for intellectual curiosity. For every old blackboard there are now hundreds of new electronic computers.

The prospect of domination of the nation's scholars by Federal employment, project allocations, and the power of money is ever present—and is gravely to be regarded.

Yet, in holding scientific research and discovery in respect, as we should, we must also be alert to the equal and opposite danger that public policy could itself become the captive of a scientific-technological elite.

It is the task of statesmanship to mold, to balance, and to integrate these and other forces, new and old, within the principles of our democratic system—ever aiming toward the supreme goals of our free society. . . .

You and I—my fellow citizens—need to be strong in our faith that all nations, under God, will reach the goal of peace with justice. May we be ever unswerving in devotion to principle, confident but humble with power, diligent in pursuit of the Nations' great goals.

To all the peoples of the world, I once more give expression to America's prayerful and continuing aspiration:

We pray that peoples of all faiths, all races, all nations, may have their great human needs satisfied; that those now denied opportunity shall come to enjoy it to the full; that all who yearn for freedom may experience its spiritual blessings; that those who have freedom will understand, also, its heavy responsibilities; that all who are insensitive to the needs of others will learn charity; that the scourges of poverty, disease and ignorance will be made to disappear from the earth, and that, in the goodness of time, all peoples will come to live together in a peace guaranteed by the binding force of mutual respect and love.

Dwight Eisenhower, farewell address, January 17, 1961.

Chronology

October 14, 1890
Dwight David Eisenhower, the third of seven sons, is born to David and Ida Stover Eisenhower in Denison, Texas.

1892
The Eisenhower family moves to Abilene, Kansas.

July 1911
Eisenhower takes the entrance exams for the Naval Academy at Annapolis and the Military Academy at West Point. Although he is too old to enter Annapolis, Eisenhower is recommended for appointment to West Point by Kansas senator Joseph Bristow.

June 12, 1915
Eisenhower graduates from West Point and is commissioned as a second lieutenant of infantry in the U.S. Army. He reports for duty with the Nineteenth Infantry at Fort Sam Houston, Texas, in September.

July 1, 1916
Eisenhower marries Mamie Geneva Doud and receives his first army promotion—to first lieutenant—on the same day.

April 1917
United States declares war on Germany and enters World War I; Eisenhower is promoted to captain the following month.

September 1917
Mamie gives birth to Doud Dwight "Icky" Eisenhower, the Eisenhowers' first son; three years later "Icky" dies suddenly from scarlet fever.

August 1922
The Eisenhowers' second son, John Sheldon Doud Eisenhower, is born.

1929
The Great Depression begins.

1939
World War II begins when Germany and Russia invade Poland.

JUNE 1941
Eisenhower is appointed chief of staff for Third Army at Fort Sam Houston, where he wins attention for his bold leadership in the Louisiana Maneuvers in August and September; promoted to brigadier general (one star) in October.

DECEMBER 1941
United States enters World War II after Japanese forces attack Pearl Harbor.

FEBRUARY 1942
Eisenhower is appointed chief of the War Plans Division, War Department General Staff, and is promoted to major general (two stars) the following month.

JUNE 1942
Eisenhower is designated commanding general of the European Theater; promoted to lieutenant general (three stars) the following month.

NOVEMBER 8, 1942
Allied forces invade North Africa; Eisenhower becomes commander in chief of Allied Forces in North Africa.

1943
Eisenhower is promoted to full general (four stars) in February; in December, Eisenhower is named Supreme Commander of the Allied Expeditionary Forces.

JUNE 6, 1944
Allied forces land in Normandy on D day; Eisenhower is promoted to General of the Army (five stars) in December.

APRIL 1945

Franklin Delano Roosevelt dies and Harry S. Truman becomes the thirty-third president of the United States; in May the German High Command surrenders unconditionally to the Allies.

AUGUST 1945

The United States drops nuclear weapons on Hiroshima and Nagasaki, ending World War II; Eisenhower becomes Army Chief of Staff in November.

JUNE 1948

Eisenhower becomes president of Columbia University.

JUNE 1950

U.S. forces begin fighting in Korea after Communist-sponsored North Korean forces attack American and British-supported South Korean forces.

DECEMBER 1950

Eisenhower takes leave from Columbia University and becomes the first Supreme Allied Commander of the North Atlantic Treaty Organization (NATO).

MAY–JULY 1952

Eisenhower retires from active service and resigns his commission in order to run for president.

NOVEMBER 4, 1952

Eisenhower is elected the thirty-fourth president of the United States.

JULY 1953

The armistice ending the Korean War is signed, and the 38th parallel is established as the boundary between North and South Korea.

APRIL 1954

The Army-McCarthy hearings take place in Congress.

MAY 1954
The French are defeated by the Vietminh at Dien Bien Phu; in the United States the Supreme Court announces its unanimous decision on *Brown v. Board of Education of Topeka, Kansas.*

MAY 1955
The USSR establishes the Warsaw Pact to oppose NATO.

SEPTEMBER 1955
Eisenhower suffers a moderately severe heart attack.

DECEMBER 1955
In Montgomery, Alabama, Rosa Parks refuses to move to the back of a bus and becomes a symbol for the civil rights movement.

OCTOBER 1956
Israeli, British, and French officials plan to internationalize the Suez Canal, which Egyptian president Nasser had closed to Israeli and some Western traffic. In a stunning attack, Israeli forces strike deep into the Suez region and seize the canal. Eisenhower responds in fury and demands that the Israelis, British, and French depart from the area.

NOVEMBER 1956
Eisenhower defeats Adlai Stevenson in a landslide election.

AUGUST 1957
Congress passes the Voting Rights Bill, the first civil rights legislation in seventy-five years.

SEPTEMBER 1957
President Eisenhower sends federal troops to enforce order in Little Rock, Arkansas.

OCTOBER 4, 1957
The Soviet Union launches *Sputnik.*

1958
Nikita Khrushchev becomes prime minister of the USSR.

OCTOBER 1958

The United States establishes the National Aeronautics and Space Administration (NASA) and launches its first satellite, *Explorer I*, into space.

NOVEMBER 1958

Khrushchev provokes an international incident by announcing his "Berlin Ultimatum," in which he describes his plans to sign an early peace treaty with East Germany. The United States, Soviet Union, Great Britain, and France meet to discuss Berlin and German reunification. The conference deadlocks in August 1959, but Eisenhower resolves the conflict by inviting Khrushchev to the United States to participate in the Camp David Summit of September 1959.

MAY 1960

An American U-2 spy plane, piloted by Francis Gary Powers, is shot down over the Soviet Union and U.S. pilot Francis Gary Powers is captured.

NOVEMBER 1960

Massachusetts Democratic senator John F. Kennedy is elected thirty-fifth president of the United States.

JANUARY 1961

President Eisenhower delivers his farewell address, in which he warns the nation of a "military-industrial complex." President and Mrs. Eisenhower retire to their Gettysburg, Pennsylvania, farm. Eisenhower is returned to the active list of the Regular Army in the grade of General of the Army, his rank from December 1944.

MARCH 28, 1969

Dwight David Eisenhower dies in Walter Reed Army Hospital; his final words are "I want to go; God take me."

FOR FURTHER RESEARCH

EISENHOWER'S LIFE AND FAMILY

STEPHEN E. AMBROSE, *Ike: Abilene to Berlin; the Life of Dwight D. Eisenhower from His Childhood in Abilene, Kansas, Through His Command of the Allied Forces in Europe in World War II.* New York: Harper & Row, 1973.

LESTER DAVID AND IRENE DAVID, *Ike and Mamie: The Story of the General and His Lady.* New York: Putnam, 1981.

DWIGHT D. EISENHOWER, *The Eisenhower Diaries.* Ed. Robert H. Ferrell. New York: Norton, 1981.

JOHN D.D. EISENHOWER, *Strictly Personal.* Garden City, NY: Doubleday, 1974.

EISENHOWER AND THE MILITARY

STEPHEN E. AMBROSE, *The Supreme Commander: The War Years of General Dwight D. Eisenhower.* Garden City, NY: Doubleday, 1970.

KENNETH S. DAVIS, *Soldier of Democracy, a Biography of Dwight Eisenhower.* Garden City, NY: Doubleday, 1952.

DAVID EISENHOWER, *Eisenhower at War: 1943–1945.* New York: Random House, 1986.

DWIGHT D. EISENHOWER, *Crusade in Europe.* Garden City, NY: Doubleday, 1948.

———, *Dear General: Eisenhower's Wartime Letters to Marshall.* Ed. Patrick Hobbs. Baltimore: Johns Hopkins Press, 1971.

———, *The Papers of Dwight David Eisenhower: The War Years.* Ed. Alfred D. Chandler Jr. Volumes I–VI. Baltimore: Johns Hopkins University Press, 1970.

ANDRE MAUROIS, *Eisenhower, the Liberator.* New York: Didier, 1945.

MERLE MILLER, *Ike the Soldier: As They Knew Him*. New York: Putnam's Sons, 1987.

ERIC K.G. SIXSMITH, *Eisenhower as Military Commander*. New York: Stein & Day, 1973.

WALTER BEDELL SMITH, *Eisenhower's Six Great Decisions: Europe, 1944–1945*. New York: Longmans, Green, 1956.

EISENHOWER'S PRESIDENCY

SHERMAN ADAMS, *Firsthand Report: The Story of the Eisenhower Administration*. New York: Harper, 1961.

DEAN ALBERSTON, ED., *Eisenhower as President*. New York: Hill & Wang, 1963.

STEPHEN E. AMBROSE, *Eisenhower: Soldier and President*. New York: Simon and Schuster, 1990.

MICHAEL R. BESCHLOSS, *Eisenhower: A Centennial Life*. New York: Harper & Row, 1990.

ROBERT L. BRANYAN AND LAWRENCE H. LARSEN, EDS., *The Eisenhower Administration, 1953–1961; a Documentary History*. New York: Random House, 1971.

ROBERT J. DONOVAN, *Eisenhower: The Inside Story*. New York: Harper, 1956.

DWIGHT D. EISENHOWER, *The Papers of Dwight David Eisenhower: Columbia University*. Ed. Louis Galambos. Volumes X–XI. Baltimore: Johns Hopkins University Press, 1984.

———, *Waging Peace, 1956–1961: The White House Years*. Garden City, NY: Doubleday, 1965.

WILLIAM BRAGG EWALD, *Eisenhower the President: Crucial Days, 1951–1960*. Englewood Cliffs, NJ: Prentice-Hall, 1981.

ROBERT K. GRAY, *Eighteen Acres Under Glass*. Garden City, NY: Doubleday, 1962.

FRED I. GREENSTEIN, *The Hidden-Hand Presidency: Eisenhower as Leader*. New York: BasicBooks, 1982.

JOHN GUNTHER, *Eisenhower: The Man and the Symbol*. New York: Harper, 1952.

R. ALTON LEE, *Dwight D. Eisenhower, Soldier and Statesman*. Chicago: Nelson-Hall, 1981.

DELOS W. LOVELACE, *"Ike" Eisenhower, Statesman and Soldier of Peace*. New York: Crowell, 1957.

PETER LYON, *Eisenhower: Portrait of the Hero*. Boston: Little, Brown, 1974.

MERLO J. PUSEY, *Eisenhower, the President*. New York: Macmillan, 1956.

ELMO RICHARDSON, *The Presidency of Dwight D. Eisenhower*. Lawrence: Regents Press of Kansas, 1979.

A. MERRIMAN SMITH, *A President's Odyssey*. New York: Harper, 1961.

ELIZABETH VAN STEENWYK, *Dwight David Eisenhower, President*. New York: Walker, 1987.

EISENHOWER'S FOREIGN POLICY

CHARLES C. ALEXANDER, *Holding the Line: The Eisenhower Era, 1952–1961*. Bloomington: Indiana University Press, 1975.

FRANCES ALTMAN, *Dwight D. Eisenhower: Crusader for Peace*. Minneapolis: T.S. Denison, 1970.

MICHAEL R. BESCHLOSS, *Mayday: Eisenhower, Khrushchev, and the U-2 Affair*. New York: Harper & Row, 1986.

DAVID BERNARD CAPITANCHICK, *The Eisenhower Presidency and American Foreign Policy*. New York: Humanities Press, 1969.

ROBERT A. DIVINE, *Eisenhower and the Cold War*. New York: Oxford University Press, 1981.

RICHARD G. HEWLETT AND JACK M. HOLL, *Atoms for Peace and War, 1953–1961: Eisenhower and the Atomic Energy Commission*. Berkeley: University of California Press, 1989.

BURTON IRA KAUFMAN, *Trade and Aid: Eisenhower's Foreign Economic Policy, 1953–1961*. Baltimore: Johns Hopkins University Press, 1982.

DOUGLAS KINNARD, *President Eisenhower and Strategy Management: A Study in Defense Politics*. Lexington: University Press of Kentucky, 1977.

RICHARD A. MELANSON AND DAVID MAYERS, EDS., *Reevaluating Eisenhower: American Foreign Policy in the 1950s*. Urbana: University of Illinois Press, 1987.

DONALD NEFF, *Warriors at Suez: Eisenhower Takes America into the Middle East*. New York: Simon and Schuster, 1981.

STEPHEN C. RABE, *Eisenhower and Latin America: The Foreign Policy of Anticommunism*. Chapel Hill: University of North Carolina Press, 1988.

WALT WHITMAN ROSTOW, *Eisenhower, Kennedy, and Foreign Aid*. Austin: University of Texas Press, 1985.

———, *Europe After Stalin: Eisenhower's Three Decisions of March 11, 1953*. Austin: University of Texas Press, 1982.

———, *Open Skies: Eisenhower's Proposal of July 21, 1955*. Austin: University of Texas Press, 1982.

EDWARD HAROLD STASSEN AND MARSHALL HOUTS, *Eisenhower— Turning the World Toward Peace*. St. Paul: Merrill/Magnus, 1990.

EISENHOWER AND CIVIL RIGHTS

JOHN W. ANDERSON, *Eisenhower, Brownell, and the Congress: The Tangled Origins of the Civil Rights Bill of 1956–1957*. Tuscaloosa: University of Alabama, 1964.

DANIEL M. BERMAN, *It Is So Ordered*. New York: Norton, 1966.

ROBERT FREDRICK BURK, *The Eisenhower Administration and Black Civil Rights*. Knoxville: University of Tennessee Press, 1984.

INDEX